Learning to Pass

CLAiT Plus 2006

Design an e-presentation

Unit 5

**Ruksana Patel
& Penny Hill**

www.heinemann.co.uk
✓ Free online support
✓ Useful weblinks
✓ 24 hour online ordering

01865 888058

Heinemann

Inspiring generations

Heinemann Educational Publishers
Halley Court, Jordan Hill, Oxford OX2 8EJ
Part of Harcourt Education

Heinemann is the registered trademark of Harcourt Education Limited

Text © Ruksana Patel and Penny Hill 2006

First published 2006

10 09 08 07 06
10 9 8 7 6 5 4 3 2 1

British Library Cataloguing in Publication Data is available from the British Library on request.

10-digit ISBN: 0 43546346 2
13-digit ISBN: 978 0 43546346 5

Copyright notice

Typeset by TechType, Abingdon, Oxon
Produced by TechType

Original illustrations © Harcourt Education Limited, 2006
Cover design by Wooden Ark
Printed in the UK by Bath Press
Cover photo: © Getty Images

Acknowledgements

Every effort has been made to contact copyright holders of material reproduced in this book. Any omissions will be rectified in subsequent printings if notice is given to the publishers.

The authors would like to thank Abdul Patel, Stephe and Mur Cove for working through the book and for providing invaluable feedback. Thank you Fayaz and Fozia Roked, Brian and Rebecca Hill for their help, encouragement and support. Thank you to Gavin Fidler and Lewis Birchon for their invaluable input which has improved the quality of the book and to Lewis for his constant support, advice and patience during the production process. And finally, we would like to thank each other for 'being there for each other'.

Tel: 01865 888058   www.heinemann.co.uk

Contents

UNIT 5: Design an e-presentation

This book has been designed to cover the syllabus for Unit 5 Design an e-presentation of the OCR Level 2 Certificate/Diploma for IT Users (CLAiT Plus) and can also be used as a basis for learning the skills for the ITQ qualification. Unit 5 is one of seven optional units from the CLAiT Plus qualification.

Learning outcomes for Unit 5: Design an e-presentation

A candidate following a programme of learning leading to this unit will be able to:

- identify and use presentation software correctly
- set up a master slide
- create a presentation
- insert and manipulate data
- control a presentation
- save, print and produce support documents for a presentation.

CLAiT Plus

The OCR Level 2 Certificate/Diploma for IT Users (CLAiT Plus) is a qualification designed to recognise the skills, knowledge and understanding of IT users in employment, education or training. It aims to provide a nationally recognised standard in IT assessment that is accessible and flexible while also being reliable, consistent and valid. It is designed to fit the needs of the learner, employer and training provider.

The redeveloped qualification

CLAiT Plus has been redeveloped to produce a qualification that provides a clear progression route, from Level 1 to Level 3, at both unit level and whole qualification level. It will equip learners with the range of transferable skills necessary to meet the demands of the modern workplace, and will prepare learners for progression to further training and accreditation in IT User skills at Level 3.

The new qualification maps to the National Occupational Standards for IT users created by e-skills UK. This takes account of recent software developments and provides greater flexibility, ease of use and relevance.

Aims of the qualification

The qualification aims to develop the following:

- knowledge of IT hardware and software and the ability to operate equipment correctly and safely
- knowledge of a range of different software applications and the ability to use different applications effectively to complete complex tasks
- the ability to manage and manipulate complex documents and data in a variety of applications
- the ability to manipulate and integrate data across different applications
- the ability to enter data accurately
- skills and knowledge in contexts that are directly relevant to employment situations
- a natural progression route for candidates who have completed a Level 1 qualification or have basic computer skills.

Structure of the qualification

UNIT STATUS	UNIT TITLE
Core unit	Unit 1: Integrated e-document production
Optional units	Unit 2: Manipulating spreadsheets and graphs
	Unit 3: Creating and using a database
	Unit 4: e-publication design
	Unit 5: Design an e-presentation
	Unit 6: e-image manipulation
	Unit 7: Website creation
	Unit 8: Electronic communication

All units are equally weighted. Candidates may work towards the units in any particular order and learning programmes can be tailored to meet individual needs.

Guided learning hours

An average candidate who has the stated recommended prior learning suggested by OCR should take around 30 guided learning hours per unit to acquire the knowledge, understanding and skills necessary to pass that unit. However, this figure is for guidance only and will vary depending on individual candidates and the mode of learning.

Recommended prior learning

There are no formal requirements for CLAiT Plus, but the CLAiT Plus units assume familiarity with IT concepts at Level 1. There are no minimum entry requirements. However, it is expected that candidates will be working at around Level 2 of the National Qualifications Framework. Candidates will benefit from the development of skills assessed through the OCR Level 1 for IT Users (New CLAiT) qualification.

Candidate profile

CLAiT Plus caters for the full range of learners in IT, whether in school, college, training, further education or employment. The qualification is suitable for those who already possess basic skills in the use of IT and who wish to develop their ability further.

It is suitable for those in full-time education who wish to gain a comprehensive qualification at Level 2. It is also suitable for those following part-time courses and those in employment who wish to develop skills in one or more specialist areas in order to meet the needs of their workplace situation.

Assessment

Units 1 to 8 are assessed in a centre by a centre assessor and are then externally moderated by an OCR examiner-moderator. OCR sets the assessments, however, OCR will allow centres/candidates to produce a suitably appropriate personalised scenario and tasks which allow the candidate to achieve all assessment objectives as listed in the individual unit specifications. Candidates are allowed a notional duration of 3 hours for each assessment. If candidates do not pass an OCR-set assignment at the first attempt, they may have other attempts at a unit using a different OCR-set assignment. In order to achieve a unit pass, candidates must make no critical errors and no more than six accuracy errors. For detailed marking criteria please refer to the OCR Level 2 Certificate/Diploma for IT Users (CLAiT Plus) *Tutor's Handbook*.

Alternative forms of assessment

Centres are able to purchase Microsoft Office Specialist tests through OCR and use these as an alternative assessment method towards the following units:

MICROSOFT OFFICE SPECIALIST TEST	OCR UNIT TO BE CLAIMED
Word core	Unit 1: Integrated e-document production
Excel core	Unit 2: Manipulating spreadsheets and graphs
Access core	Unit 3: Creating and using a database
PowerPoint core	Unit 5: Design an e-presentation
Outlook core	Unit 8: Electronic communication

Certification

Candidates may achieve individual unit certificates, an OCR Level 2 Certificate for IT Users (CLAiT Plus) or an OCR Level 2 Diploma for IT Users (CLAiT Plus).

Each unit is regarded as a worthwhile achievement in its own right. Candidates have the option of achieving as many or as few units as are appropriate to their own learning needs or employment situation. Candidates will be awarded a unit certificate for each individual unit achieved.

To achieve the Level 2 Certificate for IT Users qualification, candidates are required to achieve **three** units including the core unit (Unit 1).

Candidates who achieve **five** units, including the core unit (Unit 1), will be awarded an OCR Level 2 Diploma for IT Users.

Progression

CLAiT Plus is part of a suite of qualifications in IT User skills offered by OCR. Other IT User qualifications offered by OCR are Level 1 (New CLAiT) and Level 3 (CLAiT Advanced).

Candidates who are successful in achieving accreditation at Level 2 will be able to progress to the OCR Level 3 Certificate/Diploma for IT Users. CLAiT Plus also provides a basis for progression to the NVQs which form part of the ITQ suite, NVQ Levels 1, 2 and 3 for IT Users.

Introduction to *ITQ*

This book covers the syllabus for Unit 5 of CLAiT Plus. The skills you are learning through this study are important for employment – skills in the use of IT are needed in 9 out of 10 new jobs in the UK. This foreword explains how you can make your study even more valuable. Your successful completion of this CLAiT unit can contribute to achieving an ITQ, and your progress towards an ITQ (including your completion of this CLAiT unit) can be recorded in an e-skills Passport.

The ITQ qualification and e-skills Passport

Both the ITQ and the e-skills Passport have been created by employers. The ITQ is a flexible IT User qualification and training package that can be tailored to ensure you are trained in the IT skills that you need for your job. The ITQ is the new National Vocational Qualification (NVQ) for IT Users. It forms part of the new Apprenticeship Framework for IT Users and is based on the e-skills UK National Occupational Standards.

The e-skills Passport is an online tool that helps you build your IT User skills profile. The e-skills Passport provides a simple means for you to assess the level of your IT skills, plan your ITQ and demonstrate your progress and achievements to date. It is not a qualification, nor is it a formal appraisal system but it is a means to steer you towards the right mix of training and/or qualifications that suit you and your employer. This will give you your personal record of achievement, presented in a form that is widely understand and recognised by employers.

Although the e-skills Passport provides an essential understanding of the IT User skills that you need prior to undertaking ITQ, it is also recommended before embarking on CLAIT Plus 2006. For more information visit the e-skills Passport website (www.e-skillspassport.com).

CLAiT Plus 2006 and the ITQ

CLAiT Plus 2006 units can contribute towards the optional units for the ITQ qualification at level 2 as shown in the table below. The knowledge, understanding and skills content for CLAiT Plus 2006 units are also based on the National Occupational Standards.

ITQ UNITS	CLAIT PLUS 2006 UNITS
Word processing Level 2 (WP2)	Unit 1: Integrated e-document production
Spreadsheet software Level 2 (SS2)	Unit 2: Manipulating spreadsheets and graphs
Database software Level 2 (DB2)	Unit 3: Creating and using a database
E-mail Level 2 (MAIL2)	Unit 8: Electronic communication
Presentation software Level 2 (PS2)	Unit 5: Design an e-presentation
Website software Level 2 (WEB2)	Unit 7: Website creation
Artwork and imaging software Level 2 (ART2)	Unit 6: e-image manipulation

This book covers the syllabus for Unit PS2: Presentation software Level 2. You can use other units from CLAiT Plus 2006 and New CLAiT 2006 (which are published in Heinemann's *Learning to Pass New CLAiT/CLAiT Plus 2006* series) as well as other popular IT User qualifications to count towards your ITQ.

Therefore, if you are embarking on the ITQ and you have selected this unit then this book can provide the underpinning knowledge required to help you to successfully complete the unit.

The ITQ calculator

The ITQ can be achieved at three levels. Each component unit at each level has been allocated a number of points. The tables below also show the total number of points that need to be achieved for ITQ at each level. You can select units from different levels in order to achieve the desired number of points, provided you take the mandatory unit (Make selective use of IT) and at least 60% of your unit choices are at the ITQ level that you wish to achieve.

	ITQ LEVELS		
	Level 1	Level 2	Level 3
Total required	40	100	180
Total of points to come from optional units at level of qualification	15	40	75

For example, for a Level 2 qualification:

- overall points total of 100
- 25 points come from mandatory unit
- 75 points come from optional units
- of the 75 optional points 40 must be achieved at Level 2.

ITQ internal credit matrix

UNIT TITLES	UNIT VALUES		
	Level 1	Level 2	Level 3
Mandatory unit			
Make selective use of IT	15	25	35
Optional units			
Using IT systems	5	15	25
Operate a computer	10	20	30
IT troubleshooting for users	5	15	25
IT maintenance for users	5	15	25
IT security for users	5	15	25
Use IT to exchange information	5	15	25
Internets and intranets	5	15	25
Email	5	15	25
Word processing	10	20	30
Spreadsheets	10	20	35
Databases	10	20	35
Websites	10	20	35
IT artwork and images	10	20	35
IT presentations	10	20	30
Specialist or bespoke software	10	20	30
Evaluate the impact of IT	5	15	25
Sector specific unit	10	20	30

For more information about ITQ, visit the ITQ website (www.ITQ.org.uk).

Who this book is suitable for

This book is suitable for:

- candidates working towards OCR Level 2 Certificate/Diploma for IT Users (CLAiT Plus) and OCR ITQ qualification
- use as a self-study workbook – the user should work through the book from start to finish
- tutor-assisted workshops or tutor-led groups
- individuals wanting to extend their skills of Microsoft Office PowerPoint 2003.

Although this book is based on PowerPoint 2003, it may also be suitable for users of PowerPoint 2002 (XP). Note that a few of the skills may be different and some screenshots will not be identical.

UNIT 5: Design an e-presentation

How to use this book

In Unit 5, Design an e-presentation, you will need to create a Slide Master, a Title Slide Master and a Notes Page Master. You will insert data from other applications and embed objects into a presentation.

This book is divided into five sections:

- in Section 1, you will learn how to set up slide masters
- in Section 2, you will learn how to insert and manipulate data on slides
- in Section 3, you will learn how to embed a chart, an organisation chart and a table from a spreadsheet
- in Section 4, you will learn how to insert hyperlinks and hide slides
- in Section 5, you will learn how to insert speaker's notes, set animations and save as a slide show.

You will use a software program called Microsoft Office PowerPoint 2003 which is part of Microsoft Office 2003. PowerPoint is a presentation program which allows you to create slides with images and drawings in order to produce impressive presentations easily. We will refer to it as PowerPoint from now on. Default settings in PowerPoint are assumed.

How to work through this book

This book assumes knowledge of Level 1 skills in using PowerPoint to create and edit a presentation, use a master slide and print slides, handouts and an outline view; and Level 1 presentation terms.

1 Read the explanation of a term first.

2 If there are some terms you do not understand, refer to the **Definition of terms** on page 71.

3 Work through the book in sequence so that one skill is understood before moving on to the next. This ensures understanding of the topic and prevents unnecessary mistakes.

4 Read the **▶▶ How to...** guidelines which give step-by-step instructions for each skill. Do not attempt to work through the How to... guidelines – read through each point and look at the screenshots. Make sure you understand all the instructions before moving on.

5 To make sure that you have understood how to perform a skill, work through the **Check your understanding** task following that skill. You should refer to the How to... guidelines when doing the task.

6. At the end of each section is an **Assess your skills** list. Read through these lists to find out how confident you feel about the skills that you have learned.

7. Towards the end of the book there are **Quick reference guides**, **Build-up** and **Practice tasks**. Work through each of the tasks.

8. If you need help, you may refer to the How to… guidelines or Quick reference guides while doing the Build-up tasks. Whilst working on the Practice tasks, you should feel confident enough to use only the Quick reference guides if you need support. These guides may also be used during an assessment.

A CD-ROM accompanies this book. On it are the files that you will need to use for the tasks. Instructions for copying the files are given below. The solutions for all the tasks can be found on the CD-ROM in a folder called **L2U5EP_worked**.

If you need practice on a particular skill, you may use the files from the folder **L2U5EP_worked** to complete the appropriate practice task(s).

Note: there are many ways of performing the skills covered in this book. This book will provide How to… guidelines that are proven to be easily understood by learners.

Files for this book

To work through the tasks in this book, you will need the files from the folder called **L2U5EP_files**. This folder is on the CD-ROM provided with this book. Copy this folder into your user area before you begin.

 *copy the folder L2U5EP_files from the CD-ROM*

1. Insert the CD-ROM into the CD-ROM drive of your computer.
2. Close any dialogue boxes that may open.
3. From the desktop, double-click on the **My Computer** icon.
4. Double-click on the **CD-ROM drive** icon.
5. A dialogue box will be displayed showing the contents of the CD-ROM.
6. Click once on the folder **L2U5EP_files**.
7. The folder will be highlighted.
8. In the **File and Folder Tasks** section, click on **Copy this folder**.
9. The **Copy Items** dialogue box will be displayed.

10 In this dialogue box, click on the user area where you want to copy the folder **L2U5EP_files** to.

11 Click on the **Copy** button.

12 The folder **L2U5EP_files** will be copied to your user area.

TIP!

Paste a second copy to another folder in your user area as a backup.

Preparing your work area

You are advised to prepare your user area to keep your files for Unit 5 organised.

○ Create a folder for your CLAiT Plus work.

○ In this folder, create a subfolder for all the CLAiT Plus units that you will be doing.

○ In each unit subfolder, create further subfolders. For example:

- **U5 working**: your working folder in which all working files will be saved.

- **L2U5EP_files**: the source files folder copied from the CD-ROM.

- **L2U5EP_worked**: the worked copies folder copied from the CD-ROM.

Terms and symbols used in this book

TERM	ACTION
Click	Press and release the *left* mouse button once.
Double-click	Quickly press the left mouse button *twice* then release it.
Drag	Press and hold down the left mouse button while moving the mouse.
Select	Click on an item or highlight text.
Right-click	Press the *right* mouse button once.
+	Used to indicate that two keys should be held down together.
Hover	Position the mouse pointer over an icon or menu item and pause. A Tool tip or a further menu item will appear.
→	Indicates a new instruction follows.

LEARNING OUTCOMES

In this section you will learn how to:

- set up a Slide Master
- set up a Title Master
- set up a Notes Master
- set the slide orientation
- set the style (font type, size, emphasis, alignment)
- insert headers and footers
- create a text box
- insert an image as a background
- format the background colour on a master slide
- save a presentation
- insert an image
- move, resize and crop an image
- move and delete placeholders
- close a presentation.

Many organisations have house styles. Using a master slide to place standard items and to format text consistently ensures that a presentation follows a house style and looks professional. A master slide is like a template. PowerPoint has slide masters which enable you to ensure that all items are displayed and formatted consistently. It is important to ensure that the master slides are set up correctly because they usually form the basis on which all the slides in a presentation are created.

Master slides

PowerPoint has a number of master slide layouts.

- A *Slide Master* which has a title placeholder and a main placeholder with several levels for bulleted text and footer placeholders.
- A *Title Master* which has a title and a subtitle placeholder.
- A *Notes Master*. Notes are sometimes added to a presentation as a prompt for the speaker. These speaker's notes do not display on the screen when a presentation is run.

▶▶ How to... *display the Slide Master*

1 Click on the **View** menu.

2 Click on **Master**.

3 Click on **Slide Master**.

4 The master slide will be displayed (Figure 5.1). The frames (boxes) displayed are referred to as *placeholders*.

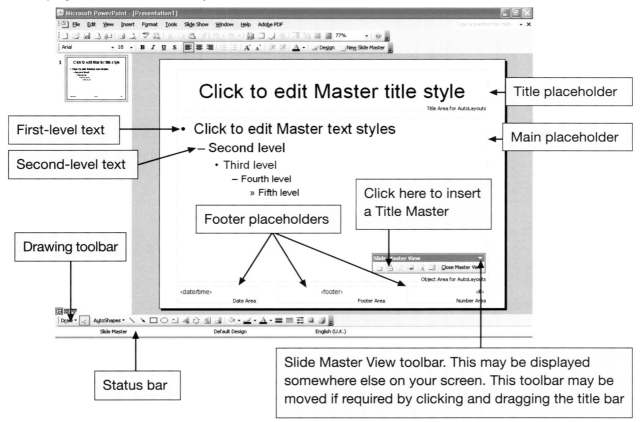

FIGURE 5.1 A master slide

Title Master

In Master view, you will not see a Title Master, but this can be inserted from the Slide Master View toolbar.

The Title Master inherits some styles, such as font type and size, from the Slide Master. However, if you make changes directly to the Title Master, those changes are always preserved and will not be affected by changes to the Slide Master.

▶▶ How to... *insert a Title Master*

1 On the Slide Master toolbar, click on the **Insert New Title Master** icon (second from the left).

2 A new Title Master will be displayed in the centre of the screen and a miniature of the Title Master will be displayed in the Slides pane on the left. Notice how the Title Master is 'linked' to the Slide Master (Figure 5.2).

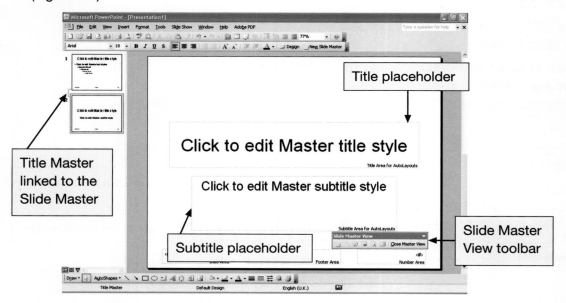

FIGURE 5.2 A Title Master slide

▶▶ How to... *display the Notes Master*

1 Click on the **View** menu.

2 Click on **Master**.

3 Click on **Notes Master** (Figure 5.3).

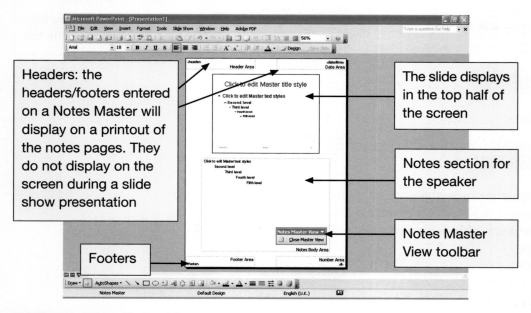

FIGURE 5.3 A Notes Master slide

▶▶ How to... *set the orientation*

1 From the **File** menu, click on **Page Setup**.

2 The **Page Setup** dialogue box will be displayed.

3 To set the slide orientation, in the **Slides** section, select **Portrait** or **Landscape**.

4 To set the orientation for notes and handouts, select **Portrait** or **Landscape** in the **Notes, handouts and outline** section.

5 Click on **OK**.

▶▶ How to... *set the style (font type, size, emphasis, alignment, colour) on a master slide*

Before you begin, ensure that the Standard and Formatting toolbars are displayed on two rows so that you can see all the icons on both toolbars. Click on the **Toolbar Options** symbol  at the right of the **Standard** toolbar. A window will be displayed. Click on **Show Buttons on Two Rows**.

1 In Slide Master view, click within the text level in the placeholder for which you want to set the style.

2 The text will be highlighted.

3 On the **Formatting** toolbar:

- Click on the drop-down arrow to the right of the **Font** box. From the drop-down list, click to select the required font type. To view the fonts further down the list, use the scroll arrow or scroll bar, *or* enter the first few letters of the required font name.
- Click on the drop-down arrow to the right of the **Font Size** box. From the drop-down list, click on the required size *or*, to set a size not displayed, enter the required size in the **Font Size** box and press **Enter**.
- Click on the icon(s) for the required emphasis (bold, italic or underline).
- Click on the icon for the required alignment (left, centre or right).
- Click on the drop-down arrow next to the **Font Color** icon and select the required colour *or* select **More Colors** and choose a colour.

Headers and footers

There are some default footer placeholders on the Slide Master. The date and any footer text can be entered directly into these placeholders or in the Header and Footer dialogue box. The default placeholders can be deleted or moved to other parts of the master slide before or after inserting headers and footers.

To insert text into headers, you can either move the existing placeholders (refer to **How to... move placeholders** on page 12) or use the **Text Box** feature 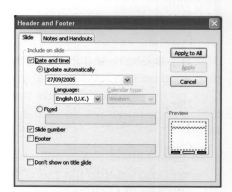 from the **Drawing** toolbar to draw text box(es) in the required position.

▶▶ How to... insert headers and footers into a master slide

If you need to insert your name and centre number, an automatic date and slide numbers into the master slide, do so via the Header and Footer dialogue box.

1 From the **View** menu, click on **Header and Footer**.

2 The **Header and Footer** dialogue box will be displayed (Figure 5.4).

3 Click to place a tick in the box for **Date and time**.

4 Click on the button for **Update automatically**.

5 Click on the drop-down arrow next to the date displayed to change the date format if required.

6 Click to place a tick in the box for **Slide number**.

7 To insert a footer, click to place a tick in the box for **Footer** and enter the footer text in the box below **Footer**.

8 Check that the **Language** box is set to **English (U.K.)**.

9 Click on **Apply to All**.

FIGURE 5.4 The Header and Footer dialogue box

When you return to Master Slide view, do not be concerned that the headers and footers do not display – these will display in Normal Slide view.

▶▶ How to... change the font size for the headers and footers

1 In Master Slide view, click on a placeholder to select it.

2 To select more than one placeholder, hold down the **Ctrl** key on the keyboard, and click on the placeholder(s).

3 On the **Formatting** toolbar, click on the drop-down arrow next to the **Font Size** box and select a size *or* enter the required size and press Enter.

▶▶ How to... create a text box on a slide

Before you begin, ensure that the Drawing toolbar is displayed. If it is not, from the **View** menu, click on **Toolbars**, then on **Drawing**.

1 On the **Drawing** toolbar, click on the **Text Box** icon ▣. The mouse pointer will change to ↓. Move your mouse to the position where you want to create the text box.

2 Click and drag the mouse to create a frame for the text box.

3 Enter the required text in the text box.

4 The default text is usually 18. Highlight the text and reduce the font size if required.

5 Check that all the text in the text box is fully displayed.

6 To change the size of a text box, click on a handle to the left or right of the box and drag to extend/reduce the size.

▶▶ How to... *insert an image as a background*

A background colour or picture applied on a Slide Master or Title Master will display on all slides in the presentation.

1 From the **Format** menu, click on **Background**.

2 The **Background** dialogue box will be displayed (Figure 5.5).

3 Click on the drop-down arrow next to the sample colour displayed.

4 Click on **Fill Effects**.

5 The **Fill Effects** dialogue box will be displayed (Figure 5.6).

6 Click on the **Picture** tab.

7 Click on the button for **Select Picture**.

8 The **Select Picture** dialogue box will be displayed (Figure 5.7).

9 Click on the drop-down arrow next to the **Look in** box. Locate the folder containing the image. Double-click to open the folder.

10 Click once on the image. Click on **Insert**.

11 The **Fill Effects** dialogue box will be displayed.

12 Click on **OK**.

13 The **Background** dialogue box will be displayed.

14 Click on **Apply to All** to display the image on all slides (or **Apply** to display the image on a selected slide).

▶▶ How to... *format the background colour*

1 From the **Format** menu, click on **Background**.

2 The **Background** dialogue box will be displayed.

3 Click on the drop-down arrow next to the sample colour displayed. A selection of colours will be displayed.

4 Click on a colour box to select a colour *or* click on **More Colors**, select a colour then click on **OK**.

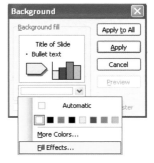

FIGURE 5.5 The Background dialogue box

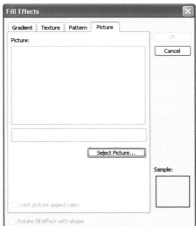

FIGURE 5.6 The Fill Effects dialogue box

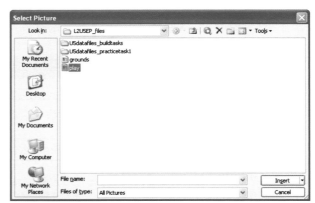

FIGURE 5.7 The Select Picture dialogue box

5 To display the background colour on the Slide Master *and* the Title Master, click on **Apply to All**. To display the background colour on the Slide Master or Title Master only select the required master from the slides pane on the left before you click on the **Format** menu. Click on **Apply**.

6 Check the Slides pane on the left. The background colour will be displayed on the master slide miniature.

▶▶ How to... *save a presentation*

1 From the **File** menu, click on **Save As**.

2 The **Save As** dialogue box will be displayed.

3 Click on the drop-down arrow to the right of the **Save in** box. Locate your user area.

4 In the **Save As** dialogue box, delete any existing text in the **File name** box. Enter the required filename. Click on **Save**.

TIP!

To save into a new folder, click on the **Create New Folder** icon. The **New Folder** box will open. Enter the new folder name. Click on **OK**.

Check your understanding *Set up a master slide*

1 Start PowerPoint and create a new presentation.

2 Display the Slide Master.

3 Set the orientation of the master slide to **landscape**.

4 Set up the master slide as follows:

BACKGROUND	TEXT FOR ALL SLIDES
Pale yellow or white	Sans serif (e.g. Berlin Sans FB, Tahoma)

ITEM	FONT	DETAIL
Header	Small	Your name and centre number
Footer	Small	Automatic date – any English format (day, month, year) Slide number to be displayed on all sides

TIP!

If font sizes are not specified, select suitable font sizes that are visibly different. For example:

Slides: large = 44 to 54, medium = 22 to 42, small = 10 to 16

Headers and footers: small = 8 to 14

Notes Pages: small = 10 to 14, medium = 18 to 24

Note: the sizes for small and medium on the slides need not be the same as the small and medium sizes for headers and footers and notes pages.

ITEM	FONT	ENHANCEMENT
Slide headings	Large	Bold
First level	Medium	Italic To include a bullet character
Second-level bullets	Smaller than first-level bullets (legible)	To include a bullet character

5 Set up the Notes Master as follows:

ITEM	FONT	DETAIL
Text	Medium	Sans serif (e.g. Berlin Sans FB, Tahoma)

6 Save the presentation using the filename **mmclub1**

7 Close the presentation.

Inserting images

As well as inserting an image as a background, you will need to learn how to insert an image into a master slide and into an individual slide.

▶▶ How to... *insert an image*

An image inserted into a master slide will be displayed on all slides in a presentation. An image inserted into an individual slide will display only on the selected slide.

1 Display the slide master or select the required slide.

2 From the **Insert** menu, click on **Picture**, then on **From File**.

3 The **Insert Picture** dialogue box will be displayed.

4 Click on the drop-down arrow next to the **Look in** box. Open the folder containing the image.

5 Click on the name of the image to be inserted.

6 Click on **Insert**.

▶▶ How to... *move an image*

1 Click once on the image to select it. White round handles will be displayed on a selected image.

2 Position the mouse on the image and drag it to the required position.

▶▶ How to... *resize an image*

1 Click once on an image to select it.

2 Position your mouse on a *corner* handle of the image.

3 The mouse pointer will change to a diagonal double-headed arrow.

4 Click and drag the double-headed arrow inwards to reduce an image size (or outwards to increase the size).

▶▶ How to... *crop an image*

1 Click once on the image to select it. Round handles will be displayed around the image.

2 The **Picture** toolbar will be displayed on the screen. If it is not, click on the **View** menu, click **Toolbar**, click on **Picture**.

3 Select the **Crop** tool ⌐ from the Picture toolbar.

4 To crop the side of an image from the top, bottom, left or right, position the mouse on the black bar at the edge of the image and drag inwards.

5 To crop the corner of an image, position the mouse on the required corner bar and drag inwards.

6 If you make a mistake, click on the **Undo** icon and start again.

What does it mean?

Crop
To crop means to cut part of an image. An image can be cropped from the top, bottom, left, right or from any of the corners.

Checking the position of items on a slide master

Once you have set the text styles, inserted any images into the master slide(s) and inserted headers and footers, you should switch to Normal view to check that items are positioned correctly and will not overlap or touch any text. If necessary, return to the master slide and make any required changes.

From the **View** menu, click on **Normal** *or* click on the button for **Close Master View** Close Master View on the Slide Master View toolbar.

▶▶ *How to...* move placeholders

1 Click on the placeholder to select it.

2 Hold down the **Ctrl** key and tap the **cursor** (arrow) key until the placeholder is moved to the required position *or* drag the placeholder to the required position.

▶▶ *How to...* delete a placeholder

1 Click on a placeholder to select it. White round handles will be displayed around it.

2 Press the **Delete** key.

▶▶ *How to...* close a presentation

1 Ensure that you have saved an updated presentation with the correct filename.

2 Click on the **File** menu.

3 Click on **Close**.

Check your understanding *Set up a Title Master*

For this task, you will need the image file **play** from the folder **L2U5EP_files**.

You will create a master slide for a presentation that will be displayed on computer screens.

1 Start PowerPoint and create a new presentation.

2 Display the **Title Slide Master**. This layout must be used for all three slides.

3 Set the slide orientation to **portrait**.

4 You may use any legible font type and size for all the slides in this presentation.

5 On the Title Master, insert the image **play** as a background for all the slides.

6 Enter your **name**, an **automatic date** and **slide numbers** as a footer on the title master slide.

7 Save the presentation using the filename **golfcomp**

ASSESS YOUR SKILLS – Set up slide masters

By working through Section 1 you will have learnt how to:

- set up a Slide Master
- set up a Title Master
- set up a Notes Master
- set the slide orientation
- set the style (font type, size, emphasis, alignment)
- insert headers and footers
- create a text box
- insert an image as a background
- format the background colour on a master slide
- save a presentation
- insert an image
- move, resize and crop an image
- move and delete placeholders
- close a presentation.

If you think that you need more practice on any of the skills in the above list, go back and work through those skills again.

If you feel confident move on to Section 2.

LEARNING OUTCOMES

In this section you will learn how to:

- ○ open a saved presentation
- ○ save an updated presentation
- ○ display Normal slide view and enter text
- ○ insert new slides
- ○ copy and paste text within a presentation
- ○ copy text from a text file and paste into a presentation
- ○ promote and demote text
- ○ spell check a presentation
- ○ delete text
- ○ delete a slide
- ○ find and replace data
- ○ print individual slides
- ○ print handouts
- ○ produce a screen print.

▶▶ How to... *open a saved presentation*

1 In PowerPoint, click on the **File** menu, click on **Open**.
2 Click on the drop-down arrow next to the **Look in** box.
3 Locate and open the folder containing the saved presentation.
4 Click on the icon for the presentation, click on **Open**.

▶▶ How to... *save an updated presentation*

From the **File** menu, click on **Save** *or* click on the **Save** icon 💾 .

▶▶ How to... *save a presentation with a new filename*

1 From the **File** menu, click on **Save As**.
2 Click on the drop-down arrow next to the **Save in** box and open your working folder.
3 In the **File name** row, delete the existing filename. Enter the new filename.
4 Click on **Save**.

1 Display the window you wish to screen print (e.g. Slide Sorter view or the Custom Animation window).

2 Press the **Print Screen** key (*or* **Alt** + **Print Screen** to capture only the active window if required).

3 Open a new Microsoft Word document (**Start**, **All Programs**, **Microsoft Office**, **Microsoft Office Word 2003**).

4 Click on the **Paste** icon *or* right-click and select **Paste** from the menu.

5 Click the **Print** icon to print the screen print.

TIP!

Remember to insert your name and centre number into all screen print documents either in the document or as a header/footer.

TIP!

You can save all your screen prints in one document and print when you have completed an assignment.

Check your understanding *Insert text and manipulate data*

For this.task you will need the following files:

theclub	text file
grounds	image
mmclub1	(that you saved earlier)

1 Using the file **mmclub1**, in Normal view check that the layout for the first slide will enable you to enter a title and a bulleted list.

2 Open the text file **theclub**.

3 Copy the prepared text to the correct slides as indicated in the text file.

4 Ensure that the formatting of the master slide is applied to all three slides.

5 On slide 1 titled **Millom Golf Society**

○ Insert the image **grounds**.

○ Reduce the image size maintaining the original proportions. Position it below the final bullet: **Challenging holes to suit all calibres**

○ Ensure that the image does not touch or overlap any text and that it is approximately centred.

6 On slide 2 titled **Membership Benefits**, demote the following bullets to second level:

To suit all levels
Men and women golfers enjoy same benefits

7 On slide 3 titled **Facilities**, demote the following bullets to second level:

Tea and coffee
Bar snacks

8 On slide 3 titled **Facilities**, below the bullet text **Bar snacks**, add the following as a second-level bullet:

Lunch and dinner

9 Replace the three instances of the word **Society** with **Club**
Maintain the use of case.

10 Save your presentation using the filename **mmclub2**

11 Print all the slides as handouts, **three** to a page.

12 Close all open files.

By working through Section 2 you will have learnt how to:

- ○ open a saved presentation
- ○ save an updated presentation
- ○ display Normal slide view and enter text
- ○ insert new slides
- ○ copy and paste text within a presentation
- ○ copy text from a text file and paste into a presentation
- ○ promote and demote text
- ○ spell check a presentation
- ○ delete text
- ○ delete a slide
- ○ find and replace data
- ○ print individual slides
- ○ print handouts
- ○ produce a screen print.

If you think that you need more practice on any of the skills in the above list, go back and work through those skills again.

If you feel confident move on to Section 3.

3: Embed a chart, organisation chart and a table

LEARNING OUTCOMES

In this section you will learn how to:

- insert a new slide into an existing presentation
- change the order of slides
- embed a chart (graph)
- enter data in the chart datasheet
- change the chart type
- add axis titles (bar charts or line graphs)
- display data labels on a pie chart
- format the chart
- use organisation charts
- embed an organisation chart
- amend boxes on an organisation chart: select and delete a box, add a subordinate, co-worker, assistant
- enter text in organisation chart boxes
- format the background colour of the boxes
- format the font for organisation charts
- insert a table from a spreadsheet
- open a provided table and copy data
- close the file containing the table
- display the table borders
- format the font type, size and emphasis in a table
- set the alignment for table cells
- set tabs in a table.

Inserting new slides into an existing presentation

A new slide will be inserted after the current slide. Therefore, before inserting a new slide, check which slide is currently selected.

 *insert a new slide into an existing presentation*

1   Check that you are in **Normal** view.

2   In the **Slides** pane on the left of the screen, click to select the slide that is *before* the position of the new slide to be inserted (Figure 5.10).

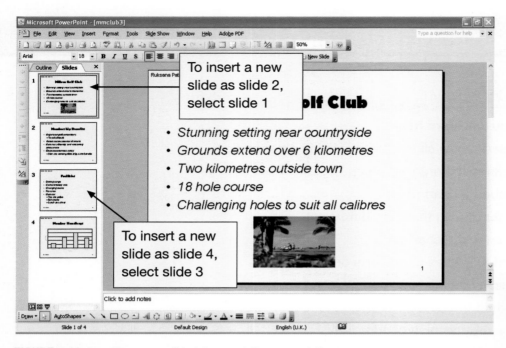

FIGURE 5.10 Inserting a new slide into an existing presentation

3 Click on the **New Slide** button ⬚ New Slide.

4 A new slide will be inserted *after* the slide that was selected.

5 In the **Slide Layout** task pane, click on the appropriate slide layout.

TIP!

If a new slide has been inserted into an incorrect position, in the Slides pane on the left, click and drag it to the required position.

▶▶ How to... *change the order of slides*

The slide order can be changed in the **Slides** pane on the left of the screen in **Normal** view or by switching to **Slide Sorter** view. To switch to Slide Sorter view, click on the **Slide Sorter View** icon.

To move slides in **Normal** or **Slide Sorter** view:

1 Click on the slide to be moved and drag it to required position *or*

2 Click once to select the slide to be moved.

3 From the **Edit** menu, click on **Cut**.

4 Click in the position *after* the slide where you want to move the slide to. A flashing line will be displayed to indicate the position. From the **Edit** menu, click on **Paste**.

▶▶ How to... *embed a chart (graph)*

1 Check that you are in **Normal** view.

2 Click on the **New Slide** button ⬚ New Slide to insert a new slide.

3 In the **Slide Layout** task pane (Figure 5.11), use the scroll bar or scroll arrow to scroll down until **Other Layouts** is visible.

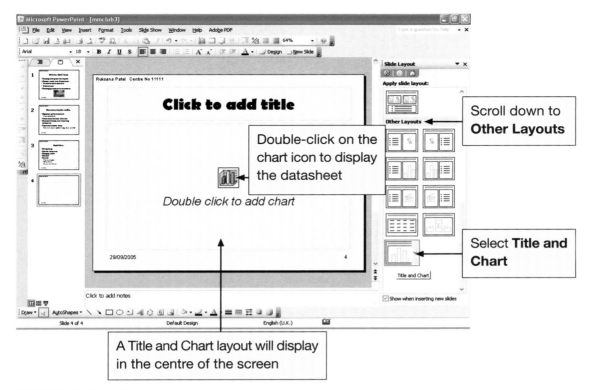

FIGURE 5.11 Embedding a chart (graph)

4 From the **Other Layouts** section, click on the **Title and Chart** layout.

5 The **Title and Chart** layout will be displayed in the centre of the screen.

6 Enter the slide title in the title placeholder.

7 In the centre of the chart, double-click on the **Chart** icon.

8 A chart Datasheet will be displayed on the screen in a separate window and a three-dimensional bar chart will display on the slide (Figure 5.12). This is the default setting in PowerPoint.

9 PowerPoint may display the Standard and Formatting toolbars on one row when you

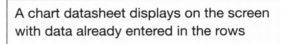

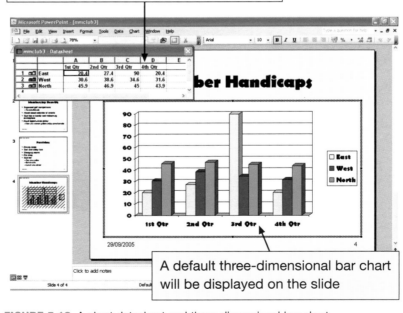

FIGURE 5.12 A chart datasheet and three-dimensional bar chart

double-click the chart icon, depending on your screen size. If so, click on the **Toolbar Options** symbol ⁝ at the right of the Standard toolbar. A window will be displayed. Click on **Show Buttons on Two Rows** (Figure 5.13).

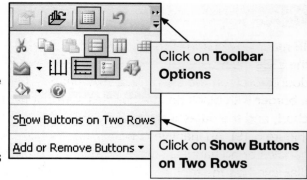

Click on **Toolbar Options**

Click on **Show Buttons on Two Rows**

FIGURE 5.13 Displaying the Standard and Formatting toolbars on two rows

▶▶ How to... *enter data in the chart datasheet*

The data in the datasheet is entered in rows by default. You will need to enter data in columns.

1 Select the entire datasheet by clicking on the top-left grey 'box' (Figure 5.14).

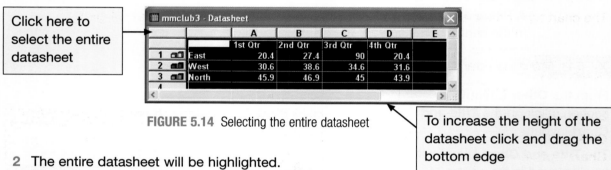

Click here to select the entire datasheet

FIGURE 5.14 Selecting the entire datasheet

To increase the height of the datasheet click and drag the bottom edge

2 The entire datasheet will be highlighted.

3 Press the **Delete** key.

4 The data in the datasheet is deleted.

5 Click on the **By Column** icon ⊞ on the **Standard** toolbar. If you do not select **By Column** your chart will not display correctly.

6 In the datasheet, click in row 1 of the first column (this column does not have a column letter).

7 Enter the data labels for the chart in the first column (Figure 5.15).

8 Click in cell **A1** (row 1, column A).

9 Enter the numbers for the chart. Ensure that you enter all numeric data with 100 per cent accuracy.

10 To widen the columns, click and drag the line between the grey column headings.

11 Click on the cross to close the datasheet.

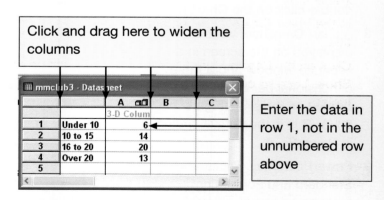

Click and drag here to widen the columns

Enter the data in row 1, not in the unnumbered row above

FIGURE 5.15 Entering the data labels and widening columns

►► How to... change the chart type

To make any changes to the chart, the chart on the slide must be active. To make a chart active, double-click on the chart. An active chart will have a border with black square handles surrounding the chart, and the datasheet will usually be displayed (Figure 5.19). An inactive chart will have white round handles or no handles surrounding it. The menus displayed on the toolbar will vary if a chart is active.

1 Ensure that the chart is active.

2 Click on the **Chart** menu and select **Chart Type**.

3 The **Chart Type** dialogue box will be displayed (Figure 5.16).

4 Select the required chart type.

5 Click on **OK**.

6 The chart type on the slide will change.

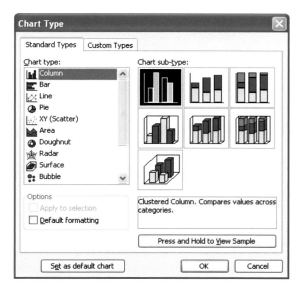

FIGURE 5.16 The Chart Type dialogue box

►► How to... add axis titles and remove the legend (bar charts or line graphs)

1 Ensure that the chart is active.

2 Click on the **Chart** menu and select **Chart Options**.

3 The **Chart Options** dialogue box will be displayed (Figure 5.17).

4 Select the **Titles** tab.

5 In the **Category (X) axis** box, enter the x-axis title.

6 In the **Value (Y) axis** box, enter the y-axis title.

7 Click on the **Legend** tab. Click in the **Show Legend** box to remove the tick (unless your chart is comparative).

8 Click on **OK**.

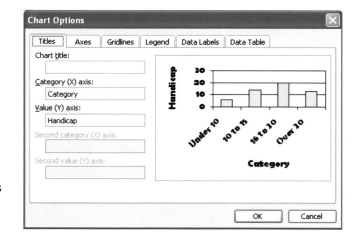

FIGURE 5.17 The Chart Options dialogue box

►► How to... display data labels on a pie chart and display/remove the legend

1 Ensure that the chart is active.

2 Click on the **Chart** menu and select **Chart Options**.

3 Select the **Data Labels** tab (Figure 5.18).

4 Tick in the boxes for the labels required.

- **Category name** to display data labels next to the sectors.
- **Value** to display numbers next to the sectors *or*
- **Percentage** to display percentages next to the sectors.

5 Click on the **Legend** tab and add/remove the tick in the **Show legend** box as required.

6 Click on **OK**.

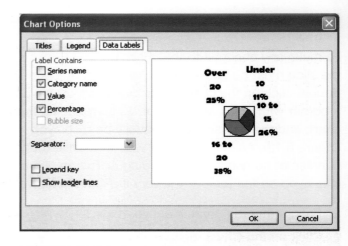

FIGURE 5.18 Selecting the Data Labels tab

▶▶ How to... *format the chart*

1 Ensure that the chart is active. Check that square handles display around the chart.

2 Click on the **Format** menu and select **Selected Chart Area** (Figure 5.19).

TIP!

If the **Selected Chart Area** option is greyed out, close the datasheet and click on the **Format** menu again.

TIP!

If the chart is not active, the option **Selected Chart Area** will not display on the **Format** menu.

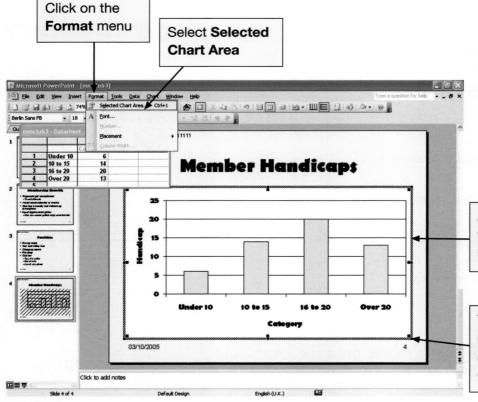

Click on the **Format** menu

Select **Selected Chart Area**

An active chart has a thick border with black square handles

To resize the chart, click on a black corner handle and drag inwards/ outwards

FIGURE 5.19 Selecting Selected Chart Area

3   The **Format Chart Area** dialogue box will be displayed (Figure 5.20).

4   Select the **Font** tab.

5   Select the required formatting.

6   Click on **OK**.

To delete the border (e.g. for pie charts), click once on the border and press the **Delete** key.

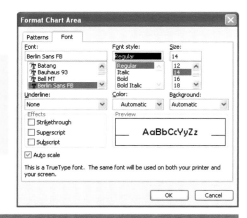

FIGURE 5.20 The Format Chart Area dialogue box

Check your understanding *Embed a chart*

1   Open your saved presentation **mmclub2** and save it using the filename **mmclub3**

2   Insert a new slide as **slide 4**.

3   Use a slide layout for slide 4 that will enable you to create a chart on the slide.

4   Insert the slide heading: **Member Handicaps**

5   Use the following data to create a **two-dimensional bar chart** on slide 4:

Under 10	**6**
10 to 15	**14**
16 to 20	**20**
Over 20	**13**

6   Title the *x*-axis **Category**

7   Title the *y*-axis **Handicap**

8   Do not display a legend.

9   Format the entire chart to be in a **sans serif** font (e.g. Arial).

10 Use any legible font size.

11 Save the presentation keeping the filename **mmclub3**.

Understanding organisation charts

Organisation charts can be used to illustrate hierarchical relationships, such as department managers and employees within a company. Look at the example shown in Figure 5.21.

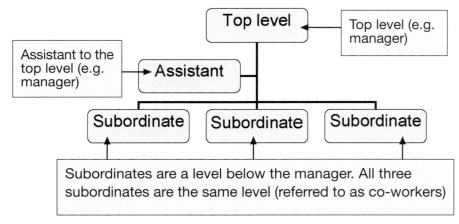

FIGURE 5.21 An organisation chart

1 Insert a new slide in the required position.

2 In the **Slide Layout** task pane, use the scroll bar or scroll arrow to scroll down until **Other Layouts** is visible.

3 From the **Other Layouts** section, click on the **Title and Diagram or Organization Chart** layout (Figure 5.22).

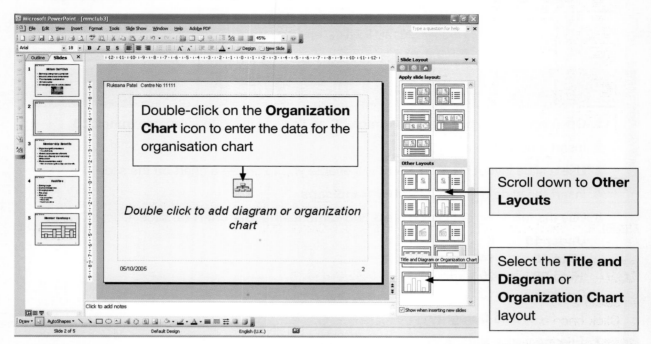

FIGURE 5.22 Embedding an organisation chart

4 The **Title and Diagram** or **Organization Chart** layout will be displayed in the centre of the screen.

5 Enter the slide heading in the title placeholder.

6 Double-click on the **Organization Chart** icon in the centre of the slide.

7 The **Diagram Gallery** dialogue box will be displayed (Figure 5.23).

8 Click on the required layout.

9 Click on **OK**.

10 A default organisation chart will display on the slide and the **Organization Chart** toolbar will be displayed on the screen (Figure 5.24).

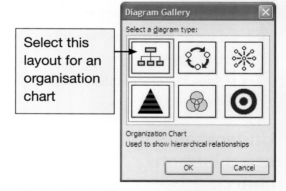

FIGURE 5.23 The Diagram Gallery dialogue box

Default organisation chart with top level and three subordinates

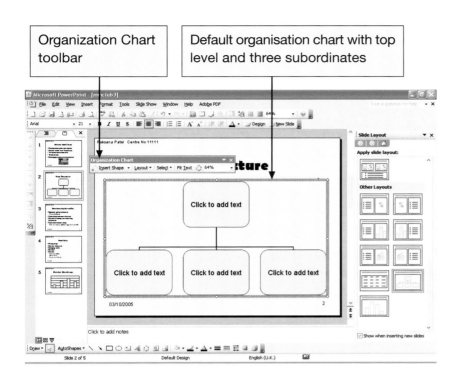

FIGURE 5.24 The default organisation chart and Organization Chart toolbar

>> **How to...** *amend boxes on an organisation chart*

To select a box:

1 Click once on the border of a box (Figure 5.25).

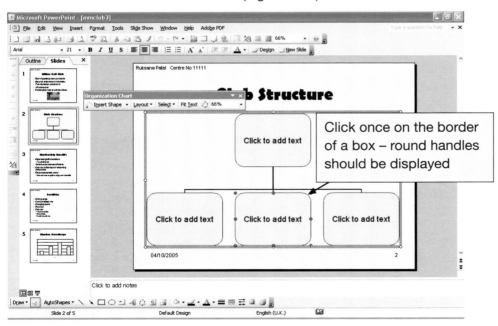

Click once on the border of a box – round handles should be displayed

FIGURE 5.25 Selecting a box

2 Round handles should display around the box. *Note:* if the handles do not display, the box has not been selected correctly. You must click on the *border*, not in the box.

To delete a box:

1 Select the box.

2 Press the **Delete** key.

TIP!

The top-level box cannot be deleted.

To add a subordinate:

1 Select the box *above* the one where the subordinate is to be added.

2 On the **Organization Chart** toolbar, click on the drop-down arrow to the right of the Insert Shape button.

3 Select **Subordinate**.

4 A new subordinate box will be added.

To add a co-worker:

Note: co-workers can only be added to the right of existing co-worker boxes by selecting an existing co-worker box.

1 Select the box for an existing co-worker.

2 Click on the drop-down arrow to the right of the Insert Shape button.

3 Select **Coworker.**

To add an assistant:

1 Select the box *above* the one where the assistant is to be added, usually the top-level box.

2 Click on the drop-down arrow to the right of the Insert Shape button.

3 Select **Assistant**.

▶▶ How to... *enter text into an organisation chart box*

1 Click in the required box.

2 Enter the required text.

3 If you need to enter a second line of text in the same box, press **Enter**.

4 Click in the next box and enter the required text. Repeat to enter the text in the remaining boxes.

▶▶ How to... *format the background colour of the boxes (optional)*

1 Select all the boxes in the organisation chart: click on the first box, hold down the **Shift** key and click on all the remaining chart boxes.

2 From the **Format** menu, click on **AutoShape**. The **Format AutoShape** dialogue box will be displayed (Figure 5.26).

3 Click on the drop-down arrow next to **Color**. Select a colour. Click on **OK**.

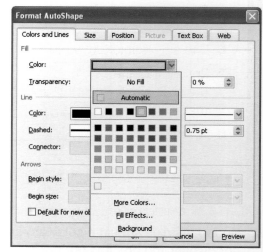

FIGURE 5.26 The Format AutoShape dialogue box

1 Select all the boxes in the organisation chart: click on the first box, hold down the **Shift** key and click on all the remaining chart boxes.

2 On the **Formatting** toolbar, click on the drop-down arrow to the right of the **Font** box. Select the required font type.

3 To change the emphasis, click on the icon for the required emphasis (e.g. bold or italic **B** *I*).

4 On the **Organization Chart** toolbar, click on Fit Text .

▶▶ **How to...** *complete an organisation chart*

1 Once you have created and formatted the chart, click outside the organisation chart placeholder. This confirms the settings.

2 Check your chart for accuracy and save the updated presentation.

3 To make any amendments to the chart, select the chart by clicking once in the chart area.

Check your understanding *Embed an organisation chart*

In your saved presentation **mmclub3**:

1 Insert a new slide as **slide 2**.

2 Use a slide layout for slide 2 that will enable you to create an organisation chart on the slide.

3 Insert the slide heading: **Club Structure**

4 Add the organisation chart shown in Figure 5.27.

5 Format the entire organisation chart to be in a **sans serif** font (e.g. Arial, Berlin Sans FB).

6 Use any legible font size.

7 Ensure that the text inside the boxes is displayed in full and that words are not split.

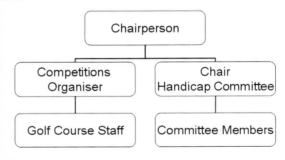

FIGURE 5.27 Organisation chart

8 You may format the font and background of the organisation chart if you wish.

9 Save your updated presentation with the filename **mmclub4**

10 Print all the slides as individual slides, **one** per page.

▶▶ How to... *insert a table from a spreadsheet*

1 Insert a new slide in the required position.

2 In the **Slide Layout** task pane, use the scroll bar or scroll arrow to scroll down to **Other Layouts**.

3 Click on the **Title and Table** layout (Figure 5.28).

4 A **Title and Table** layout will be displayed in the centre of the screen.

5 Enter the slide heading in the title placeholder.

6 Double-click on the **Table** icon.

7 The **Insert Table** dialogue box will be displayed (Figure 5.29).

8 Enter the required number of columns and rows (or use the up/down arrows).

9 Click on **OK**.

10 A table layout will be displayed in the main placeholder and the **Tables and Borders** toolbar will be displayed on the screen (Figure 5.30).

11 If the toolbar does not display, from the **View** menu, click on **Toolbars**, then on **Tables and Borders**.

12 You will now need to open the file containing the table from your user area before you insert it into the presentation.

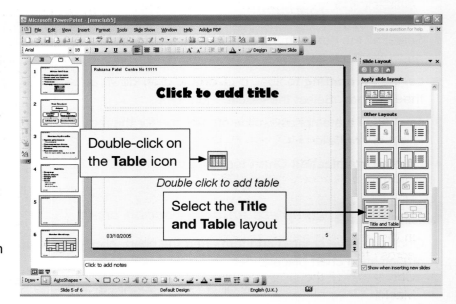

FIGURE 5.28 Inserting a table from a spreadsheet

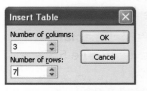

FIGURE 5.29 The Insert Table dialogue box

FIGURE 5.30 The Tables and Borders toolbar

▶▶ How to... *open a provided spreadsheet table, copy data and paste into a table on a slide*

1 Minimize the presentation by clicking on the **Minimize** icon ⬛.

2 Locate the required file in your user area.

3 Double-click on the file containing the table to open it.

4 Widen all the columns so that all the data is displayed in full: double-click between the column headings.

5 Highlight the required cells only. To highlight cells, click in the first cell, hold the **Shift** key down and click in the last cell in the range *or* click and drag across the range of cells (Figure 5.31). Do not select any additional cells.

6 From the **Edit** menu, click on **Copy** *or* click on the **Copy** icon 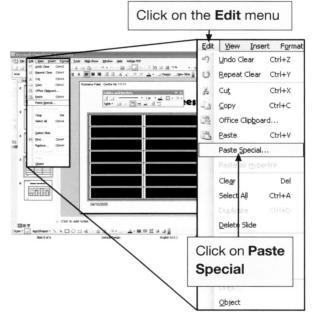.

7 A marquee (moving dotted lines) should be displayed around the selected cells.

8 Maximize the PowerPoint presentation by clicking on it once on the taskbar.

9 Highlight all the cells in the table: click in the first cell, hold the **Shift** key down and click in the last cell in the range *or* click and drag across the range of cells.

10 Check that all the cells are highlighted (usually black).

11 From the **Edit** menu, click on **Paste Special** (Figure 5.32) (do not click Paste or use the Paste icon!).

12 The **Paste Special** dialogue box will be displayed (Figure 5.33).

13 Click on **Unformatted text**.

14 Click on **OK**.

FIGURE 5.31 Highlighting the required cells

FIGURE 5.32 Clicking on Paste Special

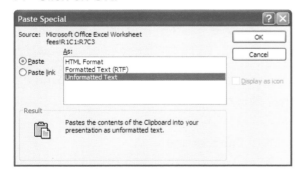

FIGURE 5.33 The Paste Special dialogue box

▶▶ How to...   *close the file containing the table*

1 On the taskbar, right-click on the icon for the file (Figure 5.34).

2 A menu will be displayed.

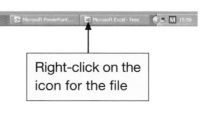

FIGURE 5.34 Closing the file containing the table

3 Click on **Close**.

4 A window will be displayed prompting you to save the changes.

5 Click on **No**.

▶▶ How to... *display table borders*

1 Highlight all the cells in the table.

2 On the **Tables and Borders** toolbar, click on the drop-down arrow next to the **Outside Borders** icon. A selection of border styles will be displayed. Click on **All Borders** (Figure 5.35).

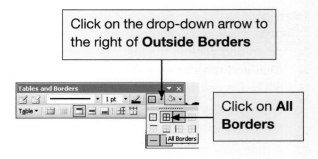

Click on the drop-down arrow to the right of **Outside Borders**

Click on **All Borders**

FIGURE 5.35 Displaying table borders

▶▶ How to... *format the font type, size and emphasis in a table*

1 Highlight all the cells in the table.

2 To set the font type, click on the drop-down arrow to the right of the **Font** box on the **Formatting** toolbar. Select the required font type.

3 To set the font size, click on the drop-down arrow to the right of the **Font Size** box on the **Formatting** toolbar. Select the required font size.

4 To set the emphasis, click on the icon for the required emphasis (e.g. bold or italic **B** *I*).

▶▶ How to... *set the alignment for table cells*

1 Highlight the relevant cells.

2 Click on the **Left**, **Center** or **Right** alignment icon ▤▤▤ on the **Formatting** toolbar.

▶▶ How to... *set tabs in a table*

1 Ensure that the ruler is displayed (from the **View** menu, click on **Ruler**). Click in the cell in which a tab is to be set.

2 The left tab ⌊ is usually displayed by default to the left of the ruler line.

3 Click on the left tab once to change it to a centre tab ⊥. Click again to change it to a right tab ⌋. Click again to change it to a decimal tab ⊥.

4 To set a tab stop in a table cell, click in the cell, then click on the ruler at the required position.

5 Repeat this process for the remaining cells in which you want to set a tab.

6 Once you have set the tab, you need to align the text to the tab stop.

7 To align text in a table to a tab stop, position the cursor in front of the text and press the **Ctrl** + **Tab** keys.

In your saved presentation **mmclub4**:

1 Insert a new slide as **slide 5**.

2 Use a slide layout for slide 5 that will enable you to insert data from a spreadsheet and display it as a table.

3 Insert the slide heading: **Club Fees**

4 Open the datafile **fees**.

5 Insert the information from this file into slide 5 as a **three-column**, **seven-row table**.

6 Display the table showing all the borders.

7 Format the entire table to a **sans serif** font (e.g. Arial, Berlin Sans FB).

8 Format the column headings **Membership**, **Type** and **Annual Fee** to **bold**.

9 Format the entire columns **Membership** and **Type** to be **left-aligned**.

10 Format the entire column **Annual Fee** to be **right-aligned**.

11 Use any legible font size.

12 Ensure all the data is displayed in full and that words are not split.

13 Save the presentation using the filename **mmclub5**

14 Print all the slides as handouts, **six** to a page.

ASSESS YOUR SKILLS – Embed a chart, organisation chart and a table

By working through Section 3 you will have learnt how to:

- insert a new slide into an existing presentation
- change the order of slides
- embed a chart (graph)
- enter data in the chart datasheet
- change the chart type
- add axis titles (bar charts or line graphs)
- display data labels on a pie chart
- format the chart
- use organisation charts
- embed an organisation chart
- amend boxes on an organisation chart: select and delete a box, add a subordinate, co-worker, assistant
- enter text in organisation chart boxes
- format the background colour of the boxes
- format the font for organisation charts
- insert a table from a spreadsheet
- open a provided table and copy data
- close the file containing the table
- display the table borders
- format the font type, size and emphasis in a table
- set the alignment for table cells
- set tabs in a table.

If you think that you need more practice on any of the skills in the above list, go back and work through those skills again.

If you feel confident move on to Section 4.

4: Insert hyperlinks and hide slides

In this section you will learn how to:

- ○ understand hidden slides
- ○ hide a slide
- ○ create a hyperlink button
- ○ edit a hyperlink button
- ○ resize a hyperlink button
- ○ move a hyperlink button
- ○ create a hyperlink using text and images
- ○ edit hyperlinked text or images
- ○ check that slides are hidden
- ○ test a hyperlink to a hidden slide.

Hidden slides

Hidden slides can be used to hide sensitive or confidential information. The hidden slide(s) can be accessed when required or can be used to extend a presentation when required.

Hidden slides are accessed via a hyperlink. An internal hyperlink can be created to display specific slides within a presentation. External hyperlinks can also be created to other documents, websites, email addresses, etc.

▶▶ How to... *hide a slide*

Slides can be hidden in the **Slides** pane in **Normal** view or in **Slide Sorter** view.

1 Select the slide to be hidden.

2 Right click with the mouse.

3 A menu will be displayed.

4 From this menu, select **Hide Slide**.

5 The slide number of a hidden slide will appear as greyed out with a diagonal line through the slide number (Figure 5.36).

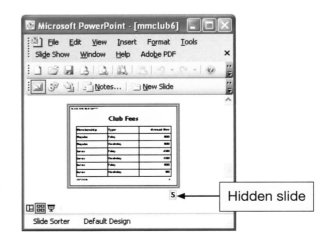

FIGURE 5.36 Hiding a slide

Hyperlinks

Hyperlinks can be created using existing text or images on the slides or by inserting a hyperlink button.

▶▶ How to... *create a hyperlink button*

1 Ensure that the slide you want to create a hyperlink button on is displayed in Normal view.

2 Click on the **Slide Show** menu.

3 Select **Action Buttons**.

4 A box will be displayed showing a range of preset action buttons (Figure 5.37).

5 Click to select any one of the buttons.

FIGURE 5.37 Preset action buttons

Creating the button:

6 Move your mouse into the area on the slide where you want to create the hyperlink. The mouse pointer changes to a cross +.

7 Do not click with the mouse!

8 Ensure that the mouse pointer is positioned in an area of the slide that will not touch or overlap any existing items on the slide.

9 Hold down the left mouse button and drag it diagonally to the right to create the button to the required size.

10 Release the mouse button.

11 The button will be created and the **Action Settings** dialogue box will be displayed (Figure 5.38).

Selecting the hidden slide to be linked:

12 In the Action Settings dialogue box, click on the **Hyperlink to** button.

13 Click on the drop-down arrow to the right of the box below **Hyperlink to**.

14 A list will be displayed.

15 Use the scroll bar or scroll arrow until you see **Slide...**

16 Click on **Slide...**

17 The **Hyperlink to Slide** dialogue box will be displayed (Figure 5.39).

FIGURE 5.38 The Action Settings dialogue box

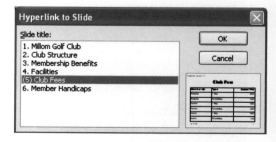

FIGURE 5.39 The Hyperlink to Slide dialogue box

18 The slide numbers and titles of all the slides in the presentation will be displayed. (*Note:* the slide number of a hidden slide will display within brackets.)

19 Click on the slide that you want to create the hyperlink to (this will usually be a hidden slide).

20 Click on **OK**.

21 The **Action Settings** dialogue box will be displayed (Figure 5.40). In the **Hyperlink to** section, the title of the linked slide will be displayed.

22 Check that this is correct.

23 Click on **OK**.

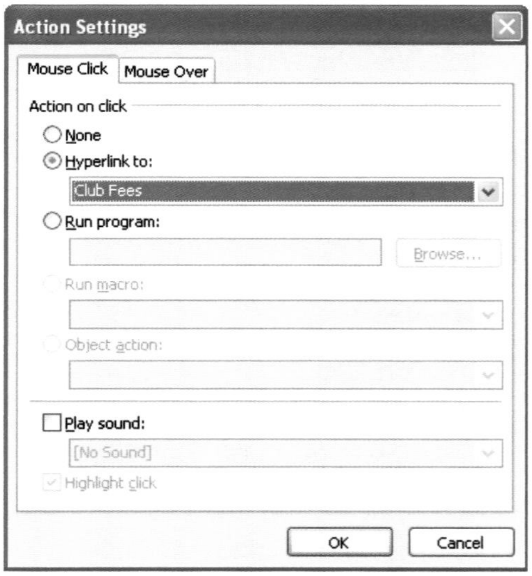

FIGURE 5.40 The Action Settings dialogue box

▶▶ How to... *edit a hyperlink button*

1 Right-click on the hyperlink button.

2 A menu will be displayed. Click on **Edit Hyperlink**.

3 Follow steps 12–23 above.

▶▶ How to... *resize a hyperlink button*

1 Click on one of the corner handles on the hyperlink button.

2 The mouse pointer will change to a double-headed arrow.

3 To reduce the size, drag the arrow inwards.

4 To increase the size, drag the arrow outwards.

▶▶ How to... *move a hyperlink button*

You must ensure that a hyperlink button does not touch or overlap any items on the slide. If it does, then the button can be easily moved.

1 Click once on the hyperlink button.

2 Hold down the left mouse button and drag the button (not the handles) to the required position, *or* hold down the **Ctrl** key and press the arrow (cursor) key.

3 Release the mouse button.

▶▶ How to... *create a hyperlink using text or images*

1 Highlight the text to be used as the link or click once to select an image.

2 Click on the **Insert** menu.

3 Click on **Hyperlink**.

TIP!

Text and images can also be linked as follows: click on the **Slide Show** menu, click **Action Settings**, select the **Hyperlink to** button, click on the drop-down arrow below **Hyperlink to** and select **Slide.....** In the **Hyperlink to Slide** dialogue box, click on the required slide, click **OK**, click **OK** again.

4 The **Insert Hyperlink** dialogue box will be displayed (Figure 5.41).

5 In the **Link to** section, click on **Place in This Document**.

6 Click on the slide to which you want to create the hyperlink.

7 Click on **OK**.

8 Click anywhere on the slide to deselect the text.

9 Note that the hyperlinked text will usually change colour and will be underlined.

FIGURE 5.41 The Insert Hyperlink dialogue box

▶▶ **How to...** *edit hyperlinked text or images*

1 Right-click on the linked image or within the linked text.

2 A menu will be displayed. Click on **Edit Hyperlink**.

3 Follow steps 5–8 above.

▶▶ **How to...** *check that slides are hidden*

Once you have created a hyperlink, you must run the presentation to ensure that the hidden slide is displayed *only* when the hyperlink is clicked. Links are tested in Slide Show view.

Run the presentation to check that the hidden slide does not display:
1 In the **Slides** pane, select **slide 1**.

2 Click on the **Slide Show** icon 🖵 at the bottom left of the screen.

3 The slide will be displayed on the full screen.

4 Check the slide number being displayed and use the **Page Down** or **down arrow** (cursor) to display the remaining slides.

5 Make sure that the hidden slide does not display.

▶▶ **How to...** *test a hyperlink to a hidden slide*

1 Display the slide with the hyperlink.

2 In **Slide Show** view, click on the hyperlink button (or hyperlinked text or image).

3 When you click on the hyperlink this should display the hidden slide.

4 Press **Esc** to end the slide show.

TIP!

If you have created a hyperlink on the wrong text or image, right-click within the linked text or image and select **Remove Hyperlink**.

Before you begin this task, make sure that you know how to delete text, how to delete a slide and how to produce screen prints. Refer to the **How to...** instructions in earlier sections if you need to.

1 Open your saved presentation **mmclub5**. Save it using the new filename **mmclub6**

2 On slide 1 titled **Millom Golf Club**, delete the entire second bullet point **Grounds extend over 6 kilometres**.

3 Ensure the bullet character and the linespace are also deleted.

4 Hide slide 5 titled **Club Fees**

You are going to create a hyperlink to link slide 4 titled **Facilities** to slide 5 titled **Club Fees** You will need to produce a screen print to provide evidence that this has been done.

Note: before you take the screen print, make sure that the slide with the hyperlink is displayed in Normal view, that the hyperlink button is clearly visible on the slide (not hidden behind dialogue boxes) and that the dialogue boxes are clearly visible. Move the dialogue boxes if required. To produce evidence of hyperlinks, you are advised to use **Print Screen** (not Alt + Print Screen).

1 On slide 4 create a hyperlink action button to link slide 4 to slide 5.

2 Take a screen print to provide evidence that the action button on slide 4 has been linked to slide 5.

3 Save this screen print using the filename **cyusp1**

4 Ensure the button does not overlap any text or lines.

5 On slide 1, select the title **Millom Golf Club**
   Create a hyperlink on this text to slide 5.

6 Take a screen print to evidence that the title **Millom Golf Club** on slide 1 has been linked to slide 5 titled **Club Fees**.

7 Paste this screen print into your saved document **cyusp1**. Enter your **name** and **centre number** in this document.

8 Test both hyperlinks to ensure that slide 5 is displayed only when the hyperlinked text on slide 1 or the hyperlink button on slide 4 is selected.

9 The chairperson has been informed that the data on the chart is not accurate. Delete slide 6 titled **Member Handicaps**.

10 Move slide 4 titled **Facilities** so that it becomes slide 2.

11 Save the presentation keeping the filename **mmclub6**

12 Print the presentation as handouts, **six** slides to a page.

13 Print the screen print document **cyusp1**

ASSESS YOUR SKILLS – Insert hyperlinks and hide slides

By working through Section 4 you will have learnt the skills how to:

○ use hidden slides

○ hide a slide

○ create a hyperlink button

○ edit a hyperlink button

○ resize a hyperlink button

○ move a hyperlink button

○ create a hyperlink using text and images

○ edit hyperlinked text or images

○ check that slides are hidden

○ test a hyperlink to a hidden slide.

If you think that you need more practice on any of the skills in the above list, go back and work through those skills again.

If you feel confident move on to Section 5.

5: Insert speaker's notes, set animations and save as slide show

LEARNING OUTCOMES

In this section you will learn how to:

○ insert speaker's notes

○ print speaker's notes

○ use animations and timings

○ set builds

○ set transitions

○ set timings

○ save a presentation as an automatic slide show

○ save a presentation for viewing without the software.

1 Ensure that the presentation is open.

2 Select the slide on which the speaker's notes are to be added.

3 From the **View** menu, click on **Notes Page**.

4 Click in the notes section below the slide.

5 Open the text file containing the speaker's notes.

6 Highlight the text to be copied. From the **Edit** menu, click on **Copy**.

7 On the taskbar, click on the presentation to maximize it.

8 Paste the copied text (Figure 5.42).

9 The formatting set on the Notes Master should be applied. If not, highlight the text and format it.

Printing speaker's notes

When speaker's notes are printed, the slide will be displayed at the top of the page and any speaker's notes will be displayed in the lower half of the page.

TIP!

Ensure that you open the correct file. You will usually have two text files.

FIGURE 5.42 Pasting the copied text into the notes page

▶▶ **How to...** *print slides with speaker's notes*

1 From the **File** menu, click on **Print**.

2 The **Print** dialogue box will be displayed (Figure 5.43).

3 In the Print dialogue box, click on the **Slides** button.

4 Enter the slide numbers to be printed, separate each number with a comma.

5 Click on the drop-down arrow to the right of the **Print what** box.

6 Select **Notes Pages**.

7 Check the **Print hidden slides** box is ticked or blank, as required.

8 Click on **OK**.

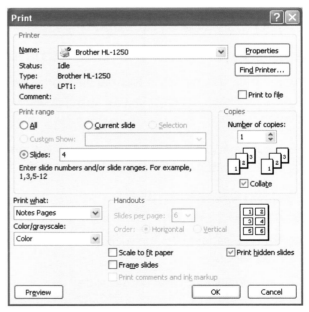

FIGURE 5.43 Printing speaker's notes

In your saved presentation **mmclub6**:

1 Select slide 4 titled **Membership Benefits**

2 Open the text file **welcome**.

3 Copy the entire text file into the notes page of slide 4.

4 Make sure that the Notes Master style has been applied to the speaker's notes.

5 Print slide 4 titled **Membership Benefits** with speaker's notes.

6 Save the presentation keeping the same filename.

Animations and timings

Animations are also referred to as builds and transitions:

○ A *build* is the direction the text appears on a new slide during a slide show presentation (e.g. it appears from the top left).

○ A *transition* is the effect that is displayed when a new slide is displayed (e.g. blinds horizontal).

○ A *timing* set on a slide determines how long the slide will display on the screen during an automatic slide show presentation.

Animations and timings can be set on individual slides or on all slides.

Setting animations and timings

Animations can be set in Normal view or Slide Sorter view. To select a slide or slides in Normal view, use the Slides pane on the left of the screen.

To set animations in Slide Sorter view, click on the **Slide Sorter View** icon 🔳 at the bottom left of the screen.

Selecting slides:

○ *All slides*: press **Ctrl** + **A** *or* click on the **Edit** menu and select **All**.

○ *Multiple slides*: click on a slide. Hold down the **Ctrl** key and click on the next slide(s).

○ *Individual slide*: click on the slide.

▶▶ How to... *set builds*

1 Select the required slides.

2 From the **Slide Show** menu, click on **Animation Schemes**.

3 The **Animation Schemes** task pane will be displayed on the right of the screen.

4   Click to set a build from the list (Figure 5.44).

5   The **Animation** icon 🌠 will be displayed under the selected slides in Slide Sorter view or to the left of the slide in the Slides pane.

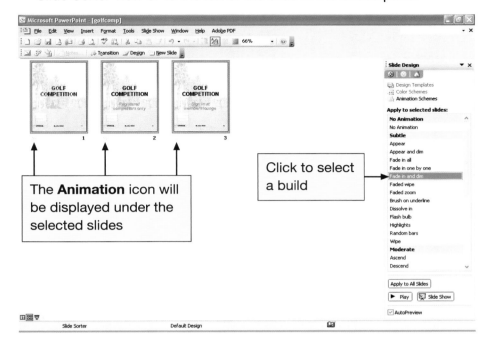

FIGURE 5.44 Setting builds

▶▶ *How to...*   *set transitions*

1   Select the required slides.

2   From the **Slide Show** menu, click on **Slide Transition**.

3   The **Slide Transition** task pane will be displayed on the right of the screen (Figure 5.45).

4   Click to set a transition from the list.

5   The **Animation** icon 🌠 will be displayed under or to the left of the selected slides (if a build has already been set, the icon does not display twice).

▶▶ *How to...*   *set timings*

1   Switch to Slide Sorter view to set timings. Select the required slides.

2   From the **Slide Show** menu, click on **Slide Transition**.

3   The **Slide Transition** task pane will be displayed on the right of the screen.

4   In the **Advance Slide** section, click in the box under **Automatically after** and enter the required timing *or* use the up/down arrows (Figure 5.45).

5   The timing will be displayed under the selected slides in Slide Sorter view. Note that timings do not display in the Slides pane.

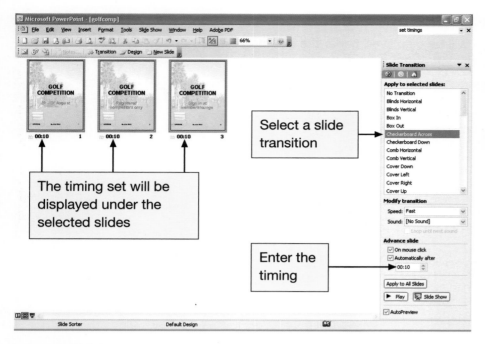

FIGURE 5.45 Setting transitions and timings

Set animations and take a screen print

In your saved presentation **mmclub6**:

1 Set an animation on slides 1 and 2.

2 Take screen print(s) to show evidence of the:

- hidden slide
- hyperlink action button
- animations set on slides 1 and 2
- order of slides.

3 Ensure the screen print(s) clearly displays all the above.

4 Ensure your **name** and **centre number** are displayed on the screen print document(s).

5 Save the screen print(s) in one document using the filename **cyusp2**

6 Print the screen print document.

7 Save the presentation keeping the same filename.

TIP!

Ensure that the slide with the hyperlink button is displayed in Normal view on the screen and that the Slides pane and the Task pane displaying the selected slides and animation are displayed on the screen before you take the screen print. This way, you should only need to take one screen print that will display all the evidence required.

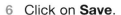 **How to...** *save a presentation as an automatic slide show*

1 From the **File** menu, click on **Save As**.

2 The **Save As** dialogue box will be displayed (Figure 5.46).

3 Click on the drop-down arrow to the right of the **Save in** box. Locate your user area/ working folder.

4 Delete any existing text in the **File name** box. Enter the required filename.

5 Click on the drop-down arrow to the right of the **Save as type** box. From the list, click on **PowerPoint Show**.

   If file extensions are displayed this will display as PowerPoint Show (.pps).

6 Click on **Save**.

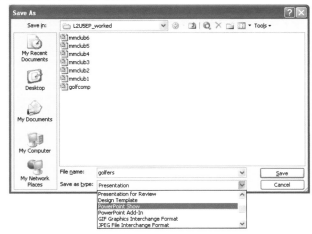

FIGURE 5.46 Saving as an automatic slide show

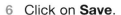 **How to...** *Save a presentation for viewing without the software*

You may need to save a presentation for viewing on another computer which does not have PowerPoint. In that case you will have to package your presentation. PowerPoint will package the presentation and other files which will then allow a user on another computer that does not have PowerPoint to run the presentation. When you package the files in PowerPoint you will not need to burn the files to a CD, so do not be concerned if you do not have CDs or CD-ROM burning software.

1 Click on the **File** menu, click on **Package for CD**. Open the presentation.

2 A **Package for CD** dialogue box displays.

3 In the **Name the CD** box, enter an appropriate name for the folder in which all the packaged files will be saved.

4 In the **Package for CD** dialogue box, click on **Copy to Folder**.

5 A **Copy to Folder** dialogue box displays.

6 In the **Location** box click the **Browse** button to locate the folder in your user area where the packaged folder is to be saved. Click on **Select** in the **Choose Location** dialogue box.

7 Click **OK** in the Copy to Folder box.

8 The files will be packaged into the folder.

9 Click **Close** to close the **Package to CD** dialogue box.

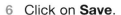 **How to...** *exit PowerPoint*

1 Click on the **File** menu.

2 Click on **Exit**.

1 Open your saved presentation **golfcomp**.

2 Set the timings and transitions as follows:

TIMINGS	TRANSITIONS
10 seconds on all slides	One transition on each slide

3 Take a screen print to show evidence that the transitions and timings have been set on all slides.

4 Save the screen print using the filename **cyusp3**

5 Print the presentation as handouts, **three** to a page. Ensure the background for each slide is visible on this printout.

6 Save the presentation in a format that will allow it to be viewed as an automatic slideshow, using the filename **golfers**

7 Take a screen print to show evidence that the file has been saved in this format. Paste the screen print in the file **cyusp3**

8 Enter your **name** and **centre number** in the file **cyusp3**

9 Print the file **cyusp3**

10 Close all open files.

11 Exit PowerPoint.

ASSESS YOUR SKILLS – Insert speaker's notes, set animations and save as slide show

By working through Section 5 you will have learnt how to:
◉ insert speaker's notes
◉ print speaker's notes
◉ use animations and timings
◉ set builds
◉ set transitions
◉ set timings
◉ save a presentation as an automatic slide show
◉ save a presentation for viewing without the software.

If you think that you need more practice on any of the skills in the above list, go back and work through those skills again.

If you feel confident do the Build-up and Practice tasks.

Keep a copy of this page next to you.
Refer to it when working through
tasks and during any assessments.

QUICK REFERENCE – Set up master slides

HOW TO...	METHOD
Start PowerPoint	Click on the Start button → click on All Programs → click on Microsoft Office → click on Microsoft PowerPoint 2003.
Create a new presentation	Click on the File menu → click on New. *Note:* a new blank presentation opens when you load PowerPoint.
Go to Slide Master view	Click on the View menu → click on Master → click on Slide Master.
Insert a Title Master	On the Slide Master toolbar → click on the icon for Insert New Title Master.
Display the Notes Page Master	Click on the View menu → click on Master → click on Notes Master.
Set the slide orientation	Click on the File menu → click on Page Setup → in the Slides section → click on Portrait or Landscape → click on OK.
Set the style (font type, emphasis, alignment, size) on a master slide	Click within the text level in the relevant placeholder → on the Formatting toolbar → click on the drop-down arrow to the right of the Font box → from the drop-down list, select the required font type → click on the drop-down arrow to the right of the Font Size box → from the drop-down list, click on the required size → click on the icon(s) for the required emphasis → click on the icon for the required alignment
Insert an image into a master slide	Click on the Insert menu → click on Picture → click on From File → the Insert Picture dialogue box will be displayed → click on the drop-down arrow next to the Look in box → go to the user area (folder) in which the image is saved → check that All pictures is displayed next to the Files of type box → in the main dialogue box, click on the name of the image to be inserted → click on Insert.
Position a graphic on a master slide	Check to see if round handles are displayed around the image → if not, click once on the image – the handles will be displayed → position the mouse anywhere within the image → the mouse pointer will change to a four-headed arrow → click and drag the image to the required position → make sure that no part of the image extends into the grey area outside the master slide.

HOW TO...	METHOD
Resize a graphic	Position the mouse on a *corner* handle of the image → the mouse will turn into a diagonal double-headed arrow → to reduce the image size: click and drag the double-headed arrow inwards → to increase the image size click and drag the double-headed arrow outwards.
Crop an image	Click once on the image to select it → round handles will be displayed on-screen → select the Crop tool from the Picture toolbar → position the mouse on the black bar at the side or corner of the image and drag inwards to crop the image.
Move footer placeholders (frames)	Click on the border of the placeholder → hold down the Ctrl key → tap the cursor (arrow) key until the placeholder is moved to the required position → repeat this process to move any other placeholders.
Check the positioning of items in Normal slide view	Click on the View menu → click on Normal.
Return to Slide Master view	Click on the View menu → click on Master → click on Slide Master.
Format the background colour	Click on the Format menu → click on Background → the Background dialogue box will be displayed → click on the drop-down arrow next to the sample colour displayed (usually white) → a selection of colours will be displayed → click on a colour box to select a colour → click on Apply to All.
Insert an image as a background	Click on the Format menu → click on Background → in the Background dialogue box → click on the drop-down arrow next to the sample colour displayed → click on Fill Effects → the Fill Effects dialogue box will be displayed → click the Picture tab → click on the button for Select Picture → the Select Picture dialogue box will be displayed → click on the drop-down arrow next to the Look in box → locate the folder containing the image → double-click to open the folder → click once on the image → click on Insert → the Fill Effects dialogue box will be displayed → click on OK → the Background dialogue box will be displayed → click on Apply to All, or Apply.
Insert text in a footer on a master slide	Click on the View menu → click on Header and Footer → the Header and Footer dialogue box will be displayed → click to place a tick in the box for Footer → enter the required text in the box below Footer.

HOW TO...	METHOD
Insert an automatic date	Click on the View menu → click on Header and Footer → the Header and Footer dialogue box will be displayed → click to place a tick in the box for Date and time → click in the button for Update automatically → click on Apply to All.
Insert slide numbers	Click on the View menu → click on Header and Footer → the Header and Footer dialogue box will be displayed → click to place a tick in the box for Slide number → click on Apply to All.
Create a text box on a master slide for header text	From the Drawing toolbar, click on the Text box icon → the mouse pointer changes to a cross → click and drag the mouse to create a frame for the text box.
Save a presentation into a new folder	Click on the File menu → click on Save As → the Save As dialogue box will be displayed → click on the down arrow to the right of the Save in box → a list of user areas will be displayed → click on your user area → click on the Create New Folder icon if required → the New Folder dialogue box will be displayed → enter the new folder name → click on OK → in the Save As dialogue box, in the File name box, delete any existing text → enter the required filename → in the Save as type box, make sure Presentation is displayed → click on the Save button.

QUICK REFERENCE – Update a presentation

Keep a copy of this page next to you. Refer to it when working through tasks and during any assessments.

HOW TO...	METHOD
Open a saved presentation	Click on the File menu → click on Open → click on the drop-down arrow next to the Look in box → go to the user area (folder) where your presentation is saved → click on the name of the presentation to be opened → click on Open.
Go to Normal slide view	Click on the View menu → click on Normal.
Insert new slides	Click on the New Slide button on the Formatting toolbar → a new slide will be displayed in the centre of the screen.
Select an appropriate slide layout	In the Text Layouts or Other Layouts pane on the right of the screen, a Slide Layout section will be displayed on the right of the screen, click on the miniature slide image for the required slide type.
Enter headings and text on slides	Click in the title placeholder → enter the required title → click in the main placeholder (frame) or the subtitle placeholder → enter the required text.
Copy and paste text within a presentation	Highlight the required text → click on the Copy icon → click in the position where the text is to be pasted → click on the Paste icon.
Copy text from a text file and paste into a presentation	Open the text file and the presentation → click on the text file on the taskbar to maximize it → highlight the text to be copied → copy it → maximize the presentation → click in the placeholder where the text is to be pasted → paste the text → maximize the text file → continue to highlight, copy and paste the remaining text.
Delete text	Place the cursor after the last character in the line → press the Backspace key → make sure the bullet character and linespace are also deleted. (Or highlight the text → press the Delete key).
Delete a slide	In Slide Sorter view or in the Slides pane → click once on the slide → press the Delete key.
Promote and demote text	Click on the Promote or Demote buttons on the Outlining toolbar or click on the Decrease Indent (to promote) or the Increase Indent (to demote) icons on the Formatting toolbar.
Spell check a presentation	Click on the Spelling and Grammar icon → if a suggestion is displayed → select it → click on Change or Ignore → click on OK.

HOW TO...	METHOD
Save a presentation with a new filename	Click on the File menu → click on Save As → the Save As dialogue box will be displayed → click on the drop-down arrow to the right of the Save in box → a list of user areas will be displayed → click on your user area → in the File name box, delete any existing text → enter the new filename → click on the Save button.
Insert text	Click in the placeholder → enter the text.
Insert a new slide into an existing presentation	In the Slides pane, click on the slide where the new slide is to be inserted (when the new slide is inserted this slide will automatically be renumbered) → click on the New Slide button on the Formatting toolbar → the Slide Layout task pane will be displayed on the right of the screen → select the required slide layout from the task pane.
Find and replace text	Click on the Edit menu → click on Replace → the Replace dialogue box will be displayed → in the Find what box, enter the word to be replaced → in the Replace with box, enter the new word → click to place a tick in the Match case box → click to place a tick in the Find whole words only box → click on Replace All → a dialogue box informing you how many replacements were made will be displayed → click on OK → click on Close.
Insert an image into a slide	Select the required slide → click on the Insert menu → click on Picture → click on From File → the Insert Picture dialogue box will be displayed → click on the drop-down arrow next to the Look in box → go to the user area (folder) in which the image is saved → check that All pictures is displayed next to the Files of type box → click on the name of the image to be inserted → click on Insert → the image will be inserted into the slide.
Change the order of slides	In the Slides pane on the left or in the Slide Sorter view → click once on the slide to be moved → drag the slide to the required position OR → click on the Edit menu → click on Cut → click with the mouse in the position after the slide where you want to move the slide to → a flashing line will be displayed to indicate the position → click on the Edit menu → click on Paste.
Save an existing presentation	Click on the File menu → click on Save (or click on the Save icon).
Print slides as individual slides	Click on the File menu → click on Print → the Print dialogue box will be displayed → click on the Slides button → in the Slides box, enter the number of each of the slides to be printed → separate each number by a comma → click on the drop-down arrow below Print what → a list will be displayed → click on Slides → check the Print hidden slides box → click on OK.

HOW TO...	METHOD
Print slides as handouts	Click on the File menu → click on Print → the Print dialogue box will be displayed → click on All or click on the Slides button → in the Slides box, enter the number of each of the slides to be printed, separate each number by a comma → click on the drop-down arrow below Print what → a list will be displayed → click on Handouts → in the Handouts section, click on the drop-down arrow next to Slides per page → click on the number required → check the Print hidden slides box → select Color below Color/grayscale → click on OK.
Print slides with speaker's notes	Click on the File menu → click on Print → in the Print dialogue box, click on the Slides button → enter the slide number(s) to be printed → separate each number with a comma → click on the drop-down arrow to the right of Print what → select Notes Pages → check the Print hidden slides box → click on OK.
Produce a screen print	Display the window you wish to screen print → press Print Screen → open Word → Paste.

Click means click with the left mouse button

Keep a copy of this page next to you. Refer to it when working through tasks and during any assessments.

QUICK REFERENCE – Embed objects

HOW TO...	METHOD
Embed a chart (graph)	In Normal view → click on the New Slide button → in the Slide Layout pane, scroll down to Other Layouts → click on Title and Chart → double-click on the Chart icon on the slide → delete all the existing data in the datasheet → click on the By Column icon → in the datasheet, click in the row numbered 1 of the first column → enter the data labels → click in cell A1 → enter the numeric data.
Select the chart type	Click on the Chart menu → select Chart Type → in the Chart Type dialogue box, select the required chart type → click on OK.
Add axis titles (bar charts or line graphs)	Ensure that the chart is active → click on the Chart menu → select Chart Options → in the Chart Options dialogue box, select the Titles tab → in the Category (X) axis box, enter the x-axis title → in the Value (Y) axis box, enter the y-axis title → click on the Legend tab → remove the tick in the Show Legend box if required → click on OK.
Display data labels on a pie chart	Ensure that the chart is active → click on the Chart menu → select Chart Options → in the Chart Options dialogue box, select Data Labels → tick in the boxes for the labels required → click on OK.
Format the chart	Ensure that the chart is active → click on the Format menu → select Selected Chart Area → the Format Chart Area dialogue box will be displayed → select the required formatting → click on OK.
Embed an organisation chart	Insert a new slide → in the Slide Layout pane, scroll down to Other Layouts → click on the Title and Diagram or Organization Chart layout → double-click on the Organisation Chart icon on the slide → in the Diagram Gallery window → click on the required layout → click on OK.
Select an organisation chart box	Click on the border of the box once → round handles will be displayed.
Delete a box	Select the box → press Delete.
Add a subordinate	Select the box for the box above the one where the subordinate is to be added → on the Organization Chart toolbar, click on the drop-down arrow to the right of Insert Shape → select Subordinate.
Add a co-worker	Select an existing co-worker box → select Insert Shape → select Coworker.

HOW TO...	METHOD
Add an assistant	Select the box for the box *above* the one where the assistant is to be added ➔ select Insert Shape ➔ select Assistant.
Enter text into an organisation chart box	Click in the box ➔ enter the required text.
Insert a table from a spreadsheet	Insert a new slide in the required position ➔ in the Slide Layout pane, scroll down to Other Layouts ➔ click on the Title and Table layout ➔ double-click on the Table icon ➔ the Insert Table dialogue box will be displayed ➔ enter the required number of columns and rows ➔ click on OK ➔ minimize the presentation ➔ open the required datafile ➔ display all data in full ➔ highlight the required cells only ➔ copy ➔ maximize the presentation ➔ highlight all the cells in the table ➔ click on the Edit menu ➔ click on Paste Special ➔ the Paste Special dialogue box will be displayed ➔ click on Unformatted text ➔ click on OK.
Display table borders	Highlight all the cells in the table ➔ on the Tables and Borders toolbar, click on the drop-down arrow next to the Outside Borders icon ➔ click on All Borders.
Format the font type, size, emphasis and alignment in a table	Highlight all the cells in the table ➔ to set the font type click on the drop-down arrow to the right of the Font box ➔ select the required font type ➔ to set the font size click on the drop-down arrow to the right of the Font Size box ➔ select a size. To set the emphasis, click on the icon for the required emphasis. To set the alignment click on the left, centre or right alignment icon.
Hide a slide	In Normal or Slide Sorter view ➔ select the slide to be hidden ➔ right-mouse click ➔ select Hide Slide from the menu ➔ the slide number will appear as greyed out.
Create a hyperlink button	Display the slide in Normal view ➔ click on the Slide Show menu ➔ select Action Buttons ➔ select a button ➔ drag the mouse to draw the shape ➔ the Action Settings dialogue box will be displayed ➔ click on the Hyperlink to button ➔ click on the drop-down arrow to the right of Hyperlink to ➔ scroll down until you see Slide... ➔ on Slide... ➔ the Hyperlink to Slide dialogue box will be displayed ➔ click on the slide that you want to create the hyperlink to ➔ click on OK ➔ click on OK to close the Action Settings dialogue box.
Create a hyperlink using text or images	Highlight the relevant text or click once to select an image ➔ click on the Insert menu ➔ click on Hyperlink ➔ in the Insert Hyperlink dialogue box, click on Place in This Document ➔ click on the slide to be linked to ➔ click on OK.

HOW TO...	METHOD
Test a hyperlink to a hidden slide	Display the slide with the hyperlink → click on the Slide Show icon → click on the hyperlink (this should display the hidden slide) → press Esc to end the slide show.
Insert speaker's notes	Select the relevant slide → click on the View menu → click on Notes Page → click in the Notes section below the slide → open the text file → highlight the text to be copied → copy → maximise the presentation → paste the copied text.
Select slides	All slides: press Ctrl + A or click on the Edit menu → select All → multiple slides: click on a slide → hold down the Ctrl key → click on the next slide(s) → individual slide: click on the slide.
Set builds	Switch to Slide Sorter view → select the required slides → click on the Slide Show menu → click on Animation Schemes → the Animation Schemes task pane will be displayed → select a build.
Set transitions	Switch to Slide Sorter view → select the required slides → click on the Slide Show menu → click on Slide Transition → the Slide Transition task pane will be displayed → select a transition.
Set timings	Switch to Slide Sorter view → select the required slides → click on the Slide Show menu → click on Slide Transition → the Slide Transition task pane will be displayed → in the Advance Slide section, click in the box under Automatically after and enter the required timing.
Save a presentation as an automatic slide show	Click on the File menu → click on Save As → click on the drop-down arrow to the right of the Save in box → locate your user area/working folder → delete any existing text in the File name box → enter the required filename → click on the drop-down arrow to the right of the Save as type box → from the list, click on PowerPoint Show → click on Save.

For this task, you will need the image file **rural** from the subfolder **U5datafiles_buildtasks**. You will create a three-slide presentation that will be displayed on computer screens.

1 Start PowerPoint and create a new presentation.

2 Select a **Title Slide** layout. This layout must be used for all three slides.

3 Set the slide orientation to **portrait**.

4 You may use any legible font type and size for all the slides in this presentation.

5 On the Title Master, insert the image **rural** as a background for all the slides. Ensure that this image fills the background.

6 Enter your **name**, an **automatic date** and **slide numbers** as a footer on the slides.

7 In Normal view, enter the text on the three title slides as shown below. The title should be entered on slide 1 and copied on to slides 2 and 3.

SLIDE	TITLE	SUBTITLE
1	Gap Year Sponsors	Teesdale and Co Accountants
2	Gap Year Sponsors	Fashion Fabric Transprinters
3	Gap Year Sponsors	Star Wholesale Supplies

8 Ensure the subtitles are displayed on two lines as shown.

9 Spell check the presentation.

10 Ensure that you have used a consistent layout for all three slides.

11 Save the presentation using the filename **sponsors**

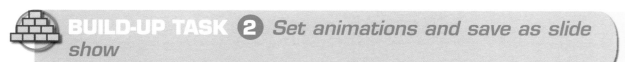
1 In your saved presentation **sponsors**

2 Set the timings and transitions as follows:

TIMINGS	TRANSITIONS
8 seconds on all slides	1 transition on each slide

3 Take a screen print to show evidence that the transitions and timings have been set on all slides.

4 Save the screen print.

5 Print the presentation as handouts, **three** to a page. Ensure that the background for each slide is visible on this printout.

6 Save the presentation in a format that will allow it to be viewed as an automatic slideshow, using the filename **gapyr**

7 Take a screen print to show evidence that the file has been saved in this format. Paste the screen print into the same document as the screen print you saved at step 4.

8 Enter your **name** and **centre number** on the screen print document.

9 Print the screen print.

10 Save and close all open files.

For this task you will need the file **cflogo**.

1 Create a new presentation.

2 Select a slide layout that will enable you to enter a title and two levels of bulleted text on each slide.

3 Set the slide orientation of the master slide to **landscape**.

4 Set up the master slide as follows:

BACKGROUND	TEXT FOR ALL SLIDES
Any pale colour or white	Sans serif (e.g. Arial)

ITEM	FONT	DETAIL
Header	Small	Your name
Footer	Small	Your centre number Automatic date – any English format (day, month, year) Slide number to be displayed on all sides

ITEM	FONT	ENHANCEMENT
Slide headings	Large	Bold
First level	Medium	Italic To include a bullet character
Second-level bullets	Smaller than first-level bullets (legible)	To include a bullet character

5 Insert the image **cflogo** at the top right of the master slide.

6 Save the presentation using the filename **careers1**

7 Set up the **Notes Master** slide as follows:

ITEM	FONT	DETAIL
Text	Medium	Sans serif (e.g. Arial)

For this task you will need the following file from the subfolder **U5datafiles_buildtasks**:

fair   text file
careers1   (that you saved earlier)

1 Using the file **careers1**, check that the layout for the first slide will enable you to enter a title and a bulleted list.

2 Open the text file **fair**.

3 Copy the prepared text on to the correct slides as indicated in the text file.

4 Ensure that the formatting of the master slide is applied to all slides.

5 On slide 1 titled **Careers Fair**, demote only the following bullets to second level:

University
Vocational courses
Army
Navy
Air Force

6 On slide 2 titled **University**, demote the following bullet to second level:

The personal statement

7 On slide 3 titled **Armed Forces**, below the bullet text **Benefits and security**, add the following as second-level bullets:

Accommodation
Health care
Pension

8 On slide 4 titled **Gap Year**, demote the following bullets to second level:

Sponsorship
Bursaries
Travel scholarships

9 Replace all instances of the word **Subjects** with **Courses**
Maintain the use of case.

10 Save your presentation using the filename **careers2**

11 Print all the slides as handouts, **four** to a page.

1 Open your saved presentation **careers2**

2 Insert a new slide as **slide 2**.

3 Use a slide layout for slide 2 that will enable you to create a chart on the slide.

4 Insert the slide heading **Previous Year Trend**

5 Use the following data to create a **two-dimensional bar chart** on slide 2:

University	**55**
College	**15**
Work	**10**
Gap year	**6**
Armed forces	**14**

6 Title the *x*-axis **Destination**

7 Title the *y*-axis **Number**

8 Do not display a legend.

9 Format the entire chart to a sans serif font (e.g. Arial).

10 Use any legible font size.

11 Save the presentation using the filename **careers3**

12 Insert a new slide as **slide 6**.

13 Use a slide layout for slide 6 that will enable you to create an organisation chart on the slide.

14 Insert the slide heading **Representatives**

15 Add the following organisation chart:

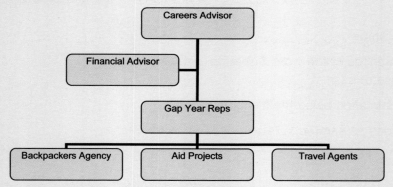

16 Format the entire organisation chart to a sans serif font (e.g. Arial).

17 Use any legible font size.

18 Ensure the text inside the boxes is displayed in full and that words are not split.

19 Save your updated presentation keeping the filename **careers3**

20 Print slides 2 and 6 as individual slides, **one** per page.

1 In your saved presentation **careers3**

2 Insert a new slide as **slide 7**.

3 Use a slide layout for slide 7 that will enable you to insert data from a spreadsheet and display it as a table.

4 Insert the slide heading **Statistics**

5 Open the datafile **genders**.

6 Insert the information from this file into slide 7 as a **three-column**, **six-row table**.

7 Display the table showing all borders.

8 Format the entire table to a **sans serif** font (e.g. Arial) and italic.

9 Format the column headings **Selection**, **Boys** and **Girls** to bold.

10 Format the entire columns **Boys** and **Girls** to be centred.

11 Use any legible font size.

12 Ensure all data is displayed in full and that words are not split.

13 On slide 4 titled **Armed Forces**, delete the entire sub-bullet point **Pension**

14 Ensure the bullet character and the linespace are also deleted.

15 Hide slide 2 titled **Previous Year Trend**.

16 Save the presentation using the filename **careers4**

17 Print slides 2 and 7 as handouts, **two** per page.

You are going to create a hyperlink to link slide 1, titled **Careers Fair**, to slide 2, titled **Previous Year Trend**. You will need to produce a screen print to evidence that this has been done.

18 On slide 1 create a hyperlink action button to link slide 1 to slide 2. Ensure the button does not overlap any text or lines.

19 Take a screen print to evidence that the action button on slide 1 has been linked to slide 2.

20 Enter your **name** and **centre number** in the screen print document.

21 Save the screen print.

22 Test the hyperlink to ensure that slide 2 is displayed only when the hyperlink button on slide 1 is selected.

23 Move slide 6 titled **Representatives** so that it becomes slide 3.

24 Save the presentation using the filename **careers5**

25 Print the presentation as handouts, **four** slides to a page.

26 Print the screen print document.

1 In your presentation **careers5**, set an animation on slides 1 and 2.

2 Take screen print(s) to show evidence of the:

hidden slide
hyperlink action button
animations set on slides 1 and 2
order of slides.

3 Ensure the screen print(s) clearly displays all the above.

4 Ensure your **name** and **centre number** are displayed on the screen print document(s).

5 Print the screen print.

6 Add speaker's notes to slide 1 titled **Careers Fair**

7 Open the text file **annual**.

8 Copy the entire text file into the notes page of slide 1.

9 Make sure that the Notes Master style has been applied to the speaker's notes.

10 Print slide 1 with speaker's notes.

11 Save your presentation using the filename **careers6**

12 Close the presentation.

13 Check your printouts for accuracy.

Scenario

You work in the office of an estate agent. You have been asked to produce two presentations, one that will advertise holiday homes and one that will be used to advertise properties for rent and for sale.

To produce the presentations you will need the following files:

FILENAME	FILE TYPE
agency	text file
details	text file
harbour	image file
home	image file
rents	datafile

During this assignment you will need to take a number of screen prints. You are advised to paste all screen prints into one document and print this document at the end of the assignment.

Task 1

In this task you will prepare master slides for the presentation that will be used to advertise the agency.

1 Select a slide layout that will enable you to enter a title and two levels of bulleted text on each slide.

2 Set the slide orientation of the master slide to **landscape**.

3 Set up the master slide as follows:

BACKGROUND	TEXT FOR ALL SLIDES
White	Sans serif (e.g. Arial, Tahoma)

ITEM	FONT	DETAIL
Header	Small	Your name and centre number
Footer	Small	Automatic date – any English format (day, month, year) Slide number to be displayed on all sides

ITEM	FONT	ENHANCEMENT
Slide headings	Large	Bold and italic
First level	Medium	No emphasis To include a bullet character
Second-level bullets	Smaller than first-level bullets (legible)	Italic To include a bullet character

4 Set up the **Notes Master** slide as follows:

ITEM	FONT	DETAIL
Text	Medium	Sans serif (e.g. Arial)

5 Save the presentation using the filename **agents1**

Task 2

Before you begin this task ensure you have the following files:

agents1 (that you saved in Task 1)
agency
home

1   Using the file **agents1**, check that the layout for the first slide will enable you to enter a title and a bulleted list.

2   Open the text file **agency**.

   Note: in the text file the words, **Slide 1**, **2**, etc., **Heading** and **1st Level Bullets** and **2nd Level Bullets** are included to show the position of the text on each slide and should *not* be included in the presentation.

3   Copy the prepared text on to the correct slides as indicated in the text file. Demote all the bullets on slide 3 to second level.

4   Ensure that the formatting of the master slide is applied to all slides.

5   On slide 3 titled **New Houses**

   a   Insert the image **home** and position this at the bottom centre of the slide.
   b   Resize the image to make it smaller, maintaining the original proportions. Ensure the image does not touch or overlap any text.

6   On slide 2 titled **Buying**, demote the following bullet to second level:

   One, two, three and four bedroom

7   On slide 3 titled **New Houses**, promote the first bullet **We feature winning developments** so that it becomes a first-level bullet.

8   On slide 4 entitled **Renting**, below the second-level bullet **Monthly leases**, add the following as a second-level bullet:

   Yearly leases

9   Replace all four instances of the word **houses** with **homes**

   Maintain the use of case.

10   Save the presentation keeping the filename **agents1**

11   Print the slides as handouts, **four** to a page.

Task 3

Before you begin this task ensure you have the following files:

agents1 (that you saved in Task 2)
rents

Some slides need to be added to the presentation. When keying in data ensure that you use the capitalisation as shown.

1 Insert a new slide as **slide 5**.

2 Use a slide layout for this slide that will enable you to insert data from a spreadsheet and display it as a table.

3 Insert the slide heading **Renting in Central London**

4 Open the datafile **rents**.

5 Insert the information from this file into the slide as a **three-column, six-row table**.

6 Display the table showing all borders.

7 Format the entire table to a **serif** font (e.g. Times New Roman).

8 Format the column headings **Type**, **Price range** and **Lease type** to bold and italic.

9 Format all data in the table to be **centre-aligned**.

10 Use any legible font size.

11 Ensure all the data is displayed in full and that words are not split.

12 Save the presentation using the filename **agents2**

13 Print the presentation as handouts, **six** slides to a page.

14 In the presentation **agents2**, insert a new slide as **slide 2**.

15 Use a slide layout for this slide that will enable you to create an organisation chart.

16 Insert the slide heading **Where to find us**

17 Add the following organisation chart:

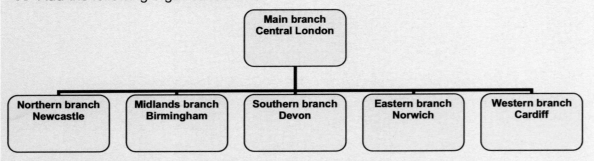

18 Format the entire organisation chart to a **serif** font (e.g. Times New Roman).

19 Use any legible font size.

20 Ensure the text inside the boxes is displayed in full and that words are not split. You may use wrapped text.

21 Insert a new slide as **slide 5**.

22 Use a slide layout for this slide that will enable you to create a chart.

23 Insert the slide heading **Wide choice of property**

24 Use the following data to create a pie chart on this slide:

Houses	**645**
Flats	**1078**
Overseas properties	**466**
Houses to let	**1200**
Flats to let	**1876**

25 Display **labels** and **percentages** next to the sectors.

26 Do not display a legend.

27 Format the entire chart to a **serif** font.

28 Use any legible font size.

29 Ensure the labels and percentages are fully displayed and that words are not split.

30 Spell check your presentation and review your work to ensure all amendments have been made.

31 Save your presentation using the filename **agents3**

32 Print the following as individual slides:

Slide 2 titled **Where to find us**
Slide 5 titled **Wide choice of property**
Slide 7 titled **Renting in Central London**

Task 4

Before you begin this task ensure you have the following file:

agents3 (that you saved in Task 3)

Some amendments need to be made to the presentation to make it suitable for viewing by a variety of audiences.

1 On **slide 1** titled **Exclusive Agents**

    a Delete the entire final bullet point **Holiday lettings**

    b Ensure the bullet character is also deleted.

2 Delete **slide 4** titled **New Homes**

3 Hide **slide 6** titled **Renting in Central London**

    You are going to create a hyperlink to link slide 5, titled **Renting**, to slide 6, titled **Renting in Central London**, and you will need to produce a screen print as evidence that this has been done.

4 On **slide 5** titled **Renting**.

    a Create a hyperlink action button to link **slide 5** to the hidden **slide 6**.

    b Take a screen print to evidence that the action button on slide 5 has been linked to slide 6 titled **Renting in Central London**

    c Save this screen print for printing later.

    d Ensure the button does not overlap with any text or lines.

    e Test the hyperlink to ensure that slide 6 is displayed only when the hyperlink button on slide 5 is selected.

5 Move **slide 2** titled **Where to find us** so that it becomes **slide 6**.

6 Set an animation on each of slides 1, 2 and 4.

7 Take a screen print to show evidence of the:

    hidden slide
    hyperlink action button
    animations set on slides 1, 2 and 4
    order of slides.

8 Ensure the screen print clearly displays all the above.

9 You may paste the screen print on to the same page as your previous screen print.

10 Ensure your **name** and **centre number** are displayed on the screen print document(s).

11 Speaker's notes need to be added to **slide 6** titled **Where to find us**

    a Set the page orientation of the speaker's notes page to **landscape**.

    b Open the text file **services**.

    c Copy the entire text file into the notes page of **slide 6**.

    d Ensure that the formatting of the Notes Master slide is applied to the notes.

    e Print **slide 6** titled **Where to find us** with speaker's notes.

12 Save your presentation using the filename **agents4**

13 Close the presentation.

Task 5

Before you begin this task ensure you have the image file **harbour**.

In this task you will create a two-slide presentation that will be displayed on a screen in a showroom.

1 Open your presentation software.

2 Create a new presentation.

3 Select a **Title Slide** layout. This layout must be used for both slides.

4 Set the slide orientation to **portrait**.

5 You may use any legible font type and size for both slides in this presentation.

6 On the Title Master slide, insert the image **harbour** as a background for both slides. Ensure this image fills the background.

7 Insert your **name** as a footer.

8 Enter the text on the two title slides as shown below:

SLIDE	TITLE	SUBTITLE
1	Summer Holiday Homes for Rent	Spain and Southern France
2	Summer Holiday Homes for Rent	Florida

9 Spell check the presentation.

10 Ensure that you have used a consistent layout for both slides.

11 Set the timings and transitions as follows:

TIMINGS	TRANSITION
5 seconds on both slides	1 transition on each slide

12 Take a screen print to show evidence that the transitions and timings have been set on all slides.

13 Ensure the timings and transitions can be clearly seen on the screen print. Ensure the background for each slide is visible on this printout.

14 Save the screen print for printing later.

15 Save the presentation using the filename **summer**

16 Print the presentation as handouts, **two** to a page.

17 Using the filename **renting**, save the presentation in a file format which will result in the presentation running immediately when opened.

18 Take a screen print to show evidence that an appropriate file format has been used.

19 You may paste the screen print on to the same page as your previous screen print.

20 Ensure your **name** and **centre number** are displayed on the screen print document(s).

21 Print this screen print and the screen prints saved earlier.

22 Save and close all open files.

UNIT 5: Design an e-presentation

Definition of terms

Amend To make changes to data. Also referred to as edit.

Animation Special effects which make text and other objects appear to move on screen.

Assistant Used in organisation charts. Someone who helps another person in an organisation.

Audience notes A handout print that displays a miniature of the slides. Also referred to as handouts.

Background The area behind text and images on slides. The background may be a solid colour, a pattern or a picture.

Builds An animation effect which controls how each bullet point or object comes into a slide.

Bullet A character in any style that is used to display a list of items.

Chart datasheet A table/spreadsheet made up of rows and columns into which data is entered to be displayed as a chart in a presentation. Data can be displayed as rows or columns.

Copy and paste A method by which text is copied from one location either in the same file or from another file and pasted into a new location. In a presentation text can be copied on to the slides and into the notes pages section of slides.

Co-worker Someone who is part of a group and who works at the same level as others within an organisation.

Crop To cut or remove part of the original image.

Data Text, numbers or images that are inserted into a presentation.

Datasheet See chart datasheet.

Delete To remove text, images or slides completely from a presentation.

Demote To indent bulleted text so that it is set further in from the left margin and becomes lower-level text.

Distort To change the original proportions (shape) of an image.

Drawing toolbar A toolbar that is usually displayed at the bottom of the screen. It includes icons for common drawing items (e.g. text boxes).

Find and Replace A technique where the computer searches for a particular word in a presentation and replaces instances of that word with an alternative word.

Folder A storage area in which files can be saved. Creating folders with suitable names allows computer files to be organised logically.

Handle Small circles that display in the corners and at the sides of a placeholder (frame) or an image. Handles are used to resize objects.

Handouts A printout displaying slides in a presentation as miniatures of the original slide size. A handout print can display 2, 3, 4, 6 or 9 slides on a page. The more slides that are displayed, the smaller the size of the miniature.

Hidden slide A slide that is not normally displayed when a presentation is run but can be accessed by clicking on hyperlinked text, image or a hyperlink button. A hidden slide may contain confidential information or information to be displayed for selective audiences only.

House style An organisation may have a prescribed style for all presentations to ensure that the background, font type, font size, font colour, etc., used in all presentations is consistent. Some organisations provide templates to ensure consistency.

Hyperlink button A button inserted on to a slide which links slides, usually to a hidden slide. Hyperlinks can also be created to other documents, websites, presentations, etc.

Import Insert a file (e.g. text or images) into a presentation from another application.

Insert slide To add a new slide to a presentation.

Marquee A moving dotted line around active cells.

Master slide A template. A master slide is used to place standard items (e.g. headers and footers and an image) and to format text consistently to ensure that a presentation looks professional.

Notes pages A PowerPoint term for speaker's notes.

Organisation chart A tree diagram which shows the ranking or levels of people who work in an organisation or a sequence of information in visual form. Often used to show the personnel structure within an organisation.

Organisation chart box The boxes into which text is entered (e.g. top level, subordinates, co-workers, assistants).

Outlining toolbar A toolbar that is usually displayed to the left of the screen. It includes the icons for Promote and Demote.

Overlap A placeholder (frame) or an image or text that touches or is partly placed above another item (e.g. text, image or placeholder).

Pane In the Normal view of PowerPoint, the screen is split into various sections referred to as panes. The left pane displays the Slides or Outline view, the bottom section displays the notes page. The main centre section displays the slide. The right section displays the task pane.

Placeholder A frame which contains text, images, headers and footers, etc. On the screen a border surrounds the placeholder – that way each placeholder (frame) can be easily seen. However, the border will not print.

Presentation A number of slides.

Promote To increase the indent of a bullet point to become a higher-level bullet point.

Sans serif This is a font family which includes a number of font types. A sans serif font type does not have any extremities or finishing strokes at the end of characters. Examples are Arial, Gill Sans.

Serif This is a font family which includes a number of font types. A serif font type has extremities or finishing strokes (curly bits!) at the end of characters. Examples are Times New Roman, Baskerville Old Face.

Slides A presentation is made up of a number of slides; each slide is displayed as a full page.

Slide layout A slide layout preset by PowerPoint. A variety of layouts can be selected. Using a preset layout for all slides helps to make sure that all text, images, footers, etc., are displayed consistently on all slides.

Slide master The term used by PowerPoint for a master slide. A slide master is used to ensure that features such as the background image or colour, font type, font size, alignment, headers and footers, etc., on each slide in a presentation are identical.

Slide show A preview of the presentation where each slide is displayed on a full screen with no menus, toolbars, etc. An audience would view a slide show with one slide displayed on a screen at a time.

Slide timings The length of time a slide will display on-screen if a presentation is run automatically.

Speaker's notes Notes that a presenter can refer to during or before the delivery of a presentation as a useful memory aid.

Task pane A section usually located on the right-hand side of the screen.

Thumbnail A miniature of a slide.

Top level The box at the top of an organisation chart, usually the most senior person (e.g. a manager).

Transition effects An animation effect which shows how one slide moves to the next one.

User area The workspace on a computer for a user to save files. Examples of user areas are the My Documents folder, a network drive, a floppy disk or the C drive.

Views Different ways of viewing a presentation on the screen. The most commonly used views are Normal, Slide Sorter and Slide Show.

General assessment guidelines for all units

Before the assessment

You are advised to obtain a copy of the syllabus from the OCR website. Read through all the assessment objectives to ensure that you have the necessary skills before you begin an assessment.

Before you start a live assessment, complete at least two 'mock exams' in assessment conditions, without help from your tutor or classmates.

The assessment

- Level 2 assessments are usually split into five or six tasks.
- You are allowed a notional duration of 3 hours for each assessment.
- Before you begin, read through the paper to see what you will need to do.
- You may want to allow yourself about 2½ hours to do all the tasks and then 30 minutes to check all your final printouts and your saved files.
- Your tutor may allow you to complete an assessment over several consecutive sessions (lessons).
- Once you start an assessment your tutor cannot give you further teaching, and is not allowed to help you, so make sure that you are ready for the assessment before you start it.
- Your tutor will provide you with a photocopy of the assignment.
- Printing can be done after the assessment, however, you are advised to print your work whenever there is an instruction to print.

TIP!

When you have printed your work, do not move straight on to the next instruction or task! Check your printout against the instructions in the assignment to make absolutely sure that you have carried out each instruction correctly and that the printout matches what you have on the screen.

During the assessment

During the assessment you are allowed to use the following:

- This Heinemann textbook that you worked through for your learning.
- The Quick reference guides from this Heinemann book.
- Your own notes.
- Handouts from your tutor that cover general IT skills.
- Any books that cover general IT skills.
- You are not allowed to use any books, notes, handouts, etc., that are referenced to the assessment objectives of the syllabus.
- You cannot ask your tutor or anyone else for help.
- If there is a technical problem (e.g. there is something wrong with the computer or printer), then you should inform your tutor or the invigilator.

- Read through the whole task before you start.
- All the instructions are numbered, and many have sub-steps (a, b, c, etc.). Read through the whole step before you do anything.
- Follow each instruction in the correct sequence. Do not leave out an instruction with the intention to do it later.
- Tick each instruction when you have completed it.
- Check that you have completed a step fully and correctly before moving on to the next step.
- Don't rush!
- Enter all the data in the same case as in the assignment.
- Enter all data as it is presented in the assignment, ignore any alternative spelling or grammar suggestions made by the software.
- Any data that you have to type in is presented in bold to help you see what you have to key in. You must not use bold emphasis unless you are told to do so in the assessment.
- Remember that, if you find an error, you can correct it, but if you leave the checking to your tutor, he or she cannot give your work back to you to correct any errors he or she has found.
- If you notice an error, you can make changes to your work and print again. You can print as many draft copies as you wish, but you must remember to destroy any incorrect copies or unwanted drafts.

You will be asked to enter your centre number. You can enter this in any format (e.g. Centre Number 11111, Centre No 11111, Centre 11111, 11111).

SAVING TIP!

Read through all the instructions for the task before you start. If you are required to save the file with a different filename, then do so before you start the task. This way you will not save over a file for the previous task.

At the end of the assessment

- Check your printouts against the assessment paper. Use a differently coloured pen/pencil to tick each instruction again in the assessment.
- Make sure you have saved all your files and have saved with the correct filename.
- Make sure all your files are saved in the correct user area and that every printout has your first and last name on it.
- Arrange your prints in the order of tasks in the assignment.
- Destroy any printouts that you do not wish to be marked (or hand these to your tutor, making sure that your tutor knows these are not to be marked).

Hand to your tutor the following:

- Your final printouts in the correct order. You may wish to staple these to keep them secure.
- The copy of the assessment paper.
- The disk you have saved your files on (if you save to disk). If not, tell the tutor where your files are saved on the computer.

Assessment guidelines for Unit 5

- Your tutor will provide you with all the files you need for the assessment.
- Before an assessment you should create a new folder just for the assessment.

TIP!

Before you start, *copy* the folder containing the files into another folder in case you need to open an original file again.

- You will usually be provided with two or three image files, two text files and a .csv file containing a table.

TIP!

Before you begin the tasks, open the text files and the csv file to familiarise yourself with the content so that you can be sure that you have inserted all the text correctly. You may wish to print these files as an aid to checking that the text has been inserted correctly.

- The order of the tasks will vary from paper to paper. You will usually need to create two presentations. In one presentation, usually the smaller presentation, you will need to insert an image as a background on a master slide or Title Master.

During the assessment, you will need to complete about five or six tasks.

General assessment tips

- Follow each instruction in the correct sequence. Do not leave an instruction with the intention to do it later.
- Do not enter any text in bold unless instructed. The text is presented in bold to help you to identify filenames, text to be entered and instructions.
- When asked to insert an automatic date and/or to display the slide numbers do not type the date or slide number; you must use the automatic date and the check box for slide numbers options in PowerPoint.
- Remember the saving tip. This is especially important for the larger presentation – you want to avoid accidentally saving over a previous version.

Filenames

You are advised to enter filenames using the same case as in the assignment. However, you will not be penalised if you use different case for filenames. Do not enter a full stop after a filename.

Headers and footers

Unless there is a specific instruction, you may use any font size, font type and alignment for headers and footers, but switch to Normal slide view to ensure that any headers or footers will not overlap with any slide items (e.g. text, images, chart, organisation chart, table). A small font size is usually best. Note that, if you need to create a text box for header items, PowerPoint usually defaults to size 18, so you are advised to reduce the size to approximately size 10–12.

Your name

You will be asked to enter your name. It is good practice to enter your first and last name.

Short presentation

There will usually be two tasks relating to a short presentation of approximately two or three slides.

You may need to:

- create/display the Title Master
- insert an image as a background on the Title Master
- insert headers/footers
- enter text on two or three slides
- set an animation. (*Note:* in one presentation you will be instructed to set builds and in the other animations.) In one of the presentations, you will need to set timings
- print the presentation (e.g. as handouts)
- save the presentation as an automatic slide show
- take a screen print of the saving
- take a screen print of the animations

Note that the papers will vary, so the above will not always be tested in the small presentation – some of these skills may be tested in the larger presentation

Short presentation assessment tips

- Set the specified orientation first. If you change the orientation later, you may need to reformat the text.
- The exact font type, size and alignment of the text and headers/footers may not be specified. In this case you may make your own selection.

> **TIP!**
>
> The heading on all the slides in the small presentation may be the same. To save time and to avoid possible data entry errors, you are advised to enter the heading on slide 1, format the font type, size and alignment, then copy and paste the heading on to the remaining slide(s).

- Ensure that you save the presentation with the specified filename and in the correct file format.
- Remember, when you print as handouts, if there is a background image on the slides, set the **Color/Grayscale** print option to **Color** (even if you are using a black and white printer). This way, the background image will print. If you set the option to **Pure black and white** or **Grayscale**, any background image will not print.